KT-405-000

ENGLAND
VERSUS
SOUTH AFRICA
1955

BRUCE HARRIS

has also written

In Quest of the Ashes
With England in Australia
1937 Test Tour
Jardine Justified
Cricket Triumph 1953
Ashes Triumphant, 1954–5

The two captains, Peter May and Jack Cheetham, cut the cake
of celebration in the Oval pavilion after England had beaten South Africa
in the final Test Match and thus won the series

ENGLAND
VERSUS
SOUTH AFRICA
1955

by

BRUCE HARRIS

With Forewords by
PETER MAY
AND
JACK CHEETHAM

and with 42 Illustrations

Hutchinson's Library of Sports and Pastimes

London   Melbourne   Sydney   Auckland
Bombay   Cape Town   New York   Toronto

First published 1955

*Printed in Great Britain
by The Anchor Press, Ltd.,
Tiptree, Essex*

CONTENTS

CONTENTS

LIST OF ILLUSTRATIONS

7

FOREWORD ONE

I have just completed my first series as captain of England and it has been a memorable experience. I shall always hold a special place in my affections for the South Africans, as it was against them that I was fortunate enough to play my first Test Match.

As a record of this series I know that you will value this book from the pen of Mr. Harris, and as a cricket writer of long standing and distinguished service his opinions and judgments should be well worthy of note.

It is in fact a great pleasure for me to offer a few words of introduction to this book, which I am sure will be of interest to everyone in the cricket world.

Peter May.

FOREWORD TWO

After the Second Test Match at Lord's, many people were inclined to say that the Series was as good as over and England's margin of victory would be so great that perhaps a good deal of interest would be lost in the remaining games.

I am proud of the manner in which my team fought back until the final Test at the Oval, when the Tests were all square, and it was a fight to the finish.

I am sure that cricket lovers will be most interested in this account of the Test Matches, and in the fluctuations of the fortunes of war, which so characterise the splendid game of cricket.

Jack Cheetham.

CHAPTER I

VICTORY, BUT ONLY JUST

ENGLAND, after toil and tribulation, has conquered South Africa at cricket by three Test Match victories to two. Not until the last day of the last match did we spot the winner.

A wonderful series it has been, even though for us Englishmen, despite the victory, a slightly disappointing one. Matches have been distinguished, if not by cricket of the very highest quality, at least by even conflict, keen though friendly rivalry and scores of no more than reasonable size.

Why then the disappointment? Let us do a little high thinking on the series and its aftermath.

First, the South Africans. They must feel pleased with themselves, even in defeat. They can fly home with this comforting knowledge: the tour, coming only about two years after their drawn series in Australia, has confirmed them as a first-class power in cricket; they can hold up their heads in any country in the world where the game is played and say "We have an even chance of beating you." I know that, in theory at least, the South Africans have taken rank in the past as our cricketing peers, but we have had mental reservations about them, such as the great world powers might feel towards the weakest of their number in international politics.

Never until now had our recent visitors won more than one Test Match in a tour of England. True, they took the rubber in 1935 when the leg-spin bowler, Xenophen Balaskas, won for them at Lord's the only match finished among five; but that victory could hardly compare in merit with the two-to-three defeat of this summer. In England, until 1955, they had won only two Test Matches and in South Africa only eleven. England had won 22 overseas and 15 in England.

The series just over marks a new relationship between the countries. The English side, due to go to the Union in the autumn of 1956, will embark with the knowledge that they have indeed a hard nut to crack. South Africa, on the whole, are a young side—only Cheetham, Endean, Mansell and Murray of the party just returning home are over 30. Their star bowlers, Tayfield, Heine, Adcock and Goddard are in their early and middle twenties; so are the batsmen who have made most runs for them, McGlew, Waite and McLean. They will be no less active in the field a year hence than now.

On the other hand, of the 25 Englishmen who had to be brought into our side to achieve their narrow victory, twelve —Appleyard, Bedser, McIntyre, Bailey, Compton, Evans, Kenyon, Wardle, Ikin, Spooner, Watson and Laker—will never see thirty again. No wonder, then, that Cheetham, at a Simpson Services Club luncheon I attended in honour of his side immediately after the fifth Test, looked forward with some eagerness to the next merry meeting.

I do not want to paint too drab a picture about the immediate future of English cricket. All I want to indicate, before the 1956 visit of the Australians to this country and our next tour in South Africa a year hence, is that all is not necessarily for the best in the best of all possible worlds.

In this southern summer of 1954–5 I had the pleasure of seeing, for the first time since my first visit to Australia in 1932–3, an English team come out on top in an Ashes struggle in Australia. When the rubber was clinched at Adelaide on 2nd February we seemed to be well established at the summit of the cricketing world for three or four years at least. We had beaten India, had drawn an exceptionally tough series in the West Indies, had "slipped" by only drawing here at home against Pakistan and had beaten Australia in England and over there.

What has happened to the winners of the greatest victory of all? The men who played in the Test series in Australia are Hutton, May, Graveney, Compton, Bailey, Cowdrey, Edrich, Appleyard, Wardle, Statham, Evans, Tyson, Simpson, Andrew and Bedser.

This side, unhappily, disintegrated in the recent English summer. Most grievous loss of all was Len Hutton, who relinquished, at least temporarily, all claims to a place in the

England side. One can only hope that his withdrawal will be only temporary, for no one is in the offing to take his place as a long-service dependable opening batsman. He tells me that he wants to have "another go" at the Australians next year and will do so if the rheumatism which afflicts him ceases to be an ally to the opposition. But there is no telling, and Hutton next year will be 40.

Compton, 38 next May, has a sick knee which bothers him all too often. Good though his form has been in the recent season when the knee has allowed, no one can prophesy what will happen.

Edrich, to all appearances, has had his day as a Test cricketer. Simpson has been left out of all the recent Tests. Appleyard, best bowler of his type in England, played in one Test against South Africa and then fell out through unfitness.

Wardle is just the same good "Johnny", but may not be given a place. Bedser was chosen only for one Test and is 37. Andrew went to Australia as reserve wicketkeeper but was ignored in the series just over for two veterans in McIntyre and Spooner after Evans was injured.

Cowdrey had a very broken season, partly through his brief period of R.A.F. service, partly through injury.

On the brighter side is the maturing genius of the captain Peter May, youngest Englishman in modern times to lead his country through a Test series. Every year his strokes grow more varied; his consistency more pronounced. There is no reason to suppose, either, that Cowdrey next year will not regain the form which helped to win the Ashes in Australia. Tyson and Statham are young enough to bowl as fast and as well as ever if they can avoid the strains and injuries which allowed them to bowl in company during only one of the recent Tests. And in Close, Yorkshire and England seem to have "got something" in the way of an opening batsman. This young left-hander, who played his first Test Match when only 18, had an unsatisfactory tour in Australia in 1950–1 and then went into the cricket wilderness, seems now to have cut out the loose strokes on the leg side by which he used to throw away his wicket. Tony Lock's bowling and fielding are an expanding asset.

One goes on hoping, year after year, that Tom Graveney will settle down into reliability as a member of the English side. Goodness knows he has had plenty of chances; he was lucky to hold his place in the 1955 side with Test scores of 42, 15, 60, 0, 1, 10 and 36 to commend him up to the eve of the fifth Test. He was chosen for that big occasion and in this low-scoring match justified himself with 13 and 42. Graveney is naturally so gifted as cricketer—not to mention golfer—that he ought to be keeping close company with May. But there is too much "if" about him when he seems to be going well. If he really can settle down then much of the problem of our middle batting is solved.

I do not believe that Graveney will ever be the ideal opener; his place is lower down the list. There *is* such a gentleman in existence, no more than 26 years of age, but with a vocation taking him away from first-class cricket. I refer, of course, to David Sheppard, of Cambridge University, Sussex and England, who showed his continued aptitude for the game whenever during last summer he snatched off time from his Divinity School at Cambridge to play a few games for Sussex. If Sheppard could have a full season's cricket in 1956 then half of the problem of our openers could be solved.

Sheppard, taking Orders in the church to which I myself am privileged to belong, is to work, we are told, in a parish in Islington. I submit, with all due respect, to his future vicar and the new deacon that nothing but good could come to that parish if Sheppard were to play again for England. The Sunday after a century against Australia at Lord's, only two or three miles away from Islington, would bring such a congregation to the church as, unfortunately, few churches nowadays attract. Any Boy Scout Troop or Youth Club having a current England opening batsman as its leader would flourish like a green bay tree.

The suggestion is made in no spirit of levity, but in all seriousness. If carried out Church and cricket would benefit. But there could be no half measures. "Time off" for Test Matches would not be enough. Sussex would have to be given his services too, for a place in the England side demands plentiful play.

Cricket in more spacious times was enriched by its clerical batsmen and bowlers; I should dearly like to see the name of the Rev. D. S. Sheppard added to the list. Surely nothing but good could arise from such a development.

There are England "possibles" with either scant experience of Test cricket or none at all. Ken Barrington, dropped after two not unsuccessful appearances as a batsman in the recent series, is one; Jim Parks, of Sussex, who played against Pakistan in 1954, is another—how lovely an innings did I see him play against Essex at Chelmsford recently! A maturer Fred Titmus ought to be of enormous value as an all-rounder.

All of these young men will be given experience in the coming tour by our "A" Team in Pakistan. The fact remains that our side against Australia next summer, instead of being ready-made and matured as we hoped, will have to be chosen and collected afresh. Here the Australians, heartened by their hollow victory over West Indies sides with whom we could only draw, and coming over here as a cohesive team, will have an enormous advantage.

The moral of it all then is "Wake up England if those Ashes are to remain here". And wake up, too, if the rubber so precariously won against South Africa is not to go the other way in 1956-7.

It is usually vain to speculate on might-have-beens in cricket. But one must be mentioned in any fair consideration of the recent series. I mean the broken elbow of the South African captain, Jack Cheetham, which cut down to three runs his second innings in the second Test and kept him out of the next two altogether. England won that second game by 71 runs. Would it have gone the other way if Cheetham's arm had not been placed in a sling? Who can say? It is at least possible.

That was the outstanding piece of bad luck on the field. There were two other serious injuries—to Godfrey Evans in the third Test, though this cannot be said to have cost us the match, and to Neil Adcock in the fourth, which his countrymen won with him a cripple.

Re-reading what I have written above, I feel I may be

accused of mud-throwing at our English side. It is the last urchin-like liberty that any writer who is not himself a performer ought to undertake. So easy is it to criticise, so difficult to put into practice. I am aware that, for that reason, some of the more extreme remarks of men who write about cricket are resented by the men who play it. I remember that during my first tour Maurice Leyland was sitting in the pavilion seats in New Zealand with a distinguished public entertainer now dead. Play was slow. "Now why didn't the batsman *hit* that ball?" this onlooker asked.

"Well, it's like this," was Leyland's reply, "our job is like yours; it's always easier to play from the stalls."

So, of course, it is. But anyone seeing cricket, day in day out, at home and overseas, for years on end, and charged with the duty of writing about it, must express definite opinions and be emphatic about them sometimes if he does his job properly. The trite saying that the onlooker sees most of the game may indeed be true. Let me, then, compare our present English side with a distinguished one of the past—and in doing this I am by no means copying—

> The idiot who praises with enthusiastic tone
> All centuries but this, and every country but his own.

In many ways cricket grows better as the years go by. But look at the side which won the Ashes for us in 1932-3, the last occasion when they were won by England before Hutton and his men achieved the feat. The eleven which, by winning the fourth Test Match at Brisbane, made quite sure of the Ashes was as follows:

D. R. Jardine, H. Sutcliffe, W. R. Hammond, R. E. S. Wyatt, M. Leyland, L. E. G. Ames, G. O. Allen, E. Paynter, H. Larwood, H. Verity and T. B. Mitchell.

In that same party, though not playing in that particular match, were the Nawab of Pataudi, W. Voce and W. E. Bowes, who all played in one or more of the other Tests.

Not a weak spot can one discern in that side. Even the

most modernist mind cannot say that even of the Hutton side in Australia, much less of the combinations who somehow have managed to worst South Africa. Every man down to number nine had a century in him—at Sydney in the succeeding Test Larwood, promoted to number four, did make 98.

Even to the present generation Larwood, Verity and Allen are familiar enough—by name as great bowlers in their day; Tommy Mitchell, the least known of them, was no bad leg-spinner either. As a wicketkeeper-batsman, or batsman-wicketkeeper, Leslie Ames ranks with anyone.

The side which won in Australia in 1954–5 could not compare with this lot in consistent all-round ability, every member pulling his full weight. Then how could the various collections arrayed against the South Africans? The Ashes were retained for us in Australia, under Hutton's command, chiefly by two bowlers, Statham and Tyson, and three batsmen, May, Compton and Cowdrey. At times, of course, these principals had good support from the supporting cast, but how much easier would victory have been if that support had been more powerful and frequent.

It is much the same with the series just over. May and Compton are one and two in the batting; the others far below them. The bowling has been much more competent and successes more widely distributed. Four men, Statham, Wardle, Tyson and Lock, went into double figures with their wickets.

One thing is certain: we can hardly hope to retain the Ashes unless we find two opening batsmen capable five times out of six of giving England a reasonable start. Peter May must not have to appear regularly from the pavilion gates at number three five minutes after a Test begins.

If Jackie McGlew, from Natal, had been a footballer of equal distinction to his cricket then the remedy would have been simple. A transfer fee of £30,000 to his club and the thing would have been done! If only he could have gone in first for us next year, in company with a reinvigorated Hutton, then come the three corners of the world in arms and we should have shocked them.

That, I fear, is a silly and idle dream. We have to forge

and develop our own talent. There is this to console us—that
the Australians will have their problems too. So will the
South Africans, for in the recent series their middle batting
was not beyond criticism.

Anyhow, it is possible to be too serious, too pre-occupied
over the question who will win. The main point, after all, is
that two wonderful struggles, one here in England against
Australia, the other overseas against South Africa, lie close
ahead. May the best side win—and may that side be ours!

CHAPTER II

OVERTURE AND BEGINNERS

BY tradition South Africa comes second only to Australia among the cricket adversaries of England. Anyone from the West Indies may argue that tradition is outworn and disproved by modern events, but there it is—it still exists. And when in the southern summer of 1952–3 a South African side under Jack Cheetham drew a series in Australia, winning two of the Test Matches, there was every reason why we should sit up and take notice.

So as Cheetham and Company flew in to London Airport in the middle of April, Englishmen took the prospective opposition very seriously indeed. Did it not contain, according to accounts from Australia, a collection of giant fieldsmen who could make moderate bowling first-class, and make first topgrade bowling super-first? Who could create catches not of this world? So we heard, and so we believed.

I remember my Australian friend Johnny Moyes, writer and broadcaster, describing one or two of those catches; they made my hair stand on end even straighter than usual.

The Australians usually come to England by sea; we take ship, too, when southward bound. The South Africans chose to fly because time is precious to them more than to our professional cricketers playing the game week in week out, sometimes as a sole means of livelihood. For most of their season the South Africans are just "week-end cricketers"; and as in parts of the Union there is no Sunday play they become just Saturday afternooners—except for half a dozen Currie Cup fixtures.

It is highly to their credit then that they can take their place in top-flight international cricket. What they lack in constant daily match practice they gain in enthusiasm and spontaneity. It is not altogether an advantage to play cricket six days a week for five months on end, year in year out; zest for the game is apt to be blunted. Cricket may become a job of work, to be accomplished with as little labour as possible.

Watch some of our County sides in August and that is the impression you will form. They become jaded and stale. Who shall blame them?

On the other hand these South African amateurs, released from work for a whole season of uninterrupted cricket, feel like schoolboys given an unexpected holiday. Towards the end of a strenuous tour they discover there can be too much even of a good thing like cricket; they do not love it in September as they do in May, but by that time the tour is drawing to an end.

Who were the seventeen who, with Cheetham at their head, landed in the dry sunshine of an April soon to be succeeded by the cold and wet of an inhospitable May? They were:

J. E. CHEETHAM, the captain, one of the seven "survivors" of the 1951 tour in England and captain of the half-triumphant side in Australia. Aged 34 when the tour began. Civil engineer. From Western Province. Resolute bat; fine field; inspiring leader.

D. J. McGLEW, vice-captain, 26. He was here in 1951. Scored 250 runs in eight innings in the Tests in Australia. Sports outfitter in Durban, Natal. One of the smaller members of the side. As opening batsman, lives up to the second syllable of his surname. Superb cover-point.

Now, having dealt with the two leaders, I will become alphabetical:

N. A. T. ADCOCK, 24, and not a member of either the 1951 side in England or the 1952 one in Australia. Fast bowler, for whom it was claimed that in speed he reached the Tyson standard. I did not think so. Took 24 wickets in his first series —against New Zealand in 1953. From Transvaal. Clerk.

C. A. R. DUCKWORTH, 21, youngest member of the side. Having his first tour abroad. Plays for Rhodesia. Good reserve wicketkeeper who, as a batsman during tour just over, sprang into prominence after a series of small innings by scoring 158 against Northants. Schoolmaster.

W. R. ENDEAN, 31, a "second-timer" like Cheetham and McGlew, was the star batting success in Australia—Test runs 438—average 48. Wicketkeeper who ceased to keep wicket to concentrate on batting. Scored 197 before lunch for

Transvaal against Orange Free State last South African season. Chartered accountant. International hockey player.

E. R. H. FULLER, 23, accountant. First visit to England, but was at the top of his country's Test bowling averages in Australia—ten wickets at 27. Bowls fast-medium, bats and fields well. From Cape Province.

T. L. GODDARD, 23, draughtsman. Left-hand lively medium pace bowler and left-hand bat, frequently opening in both departments. Became one of the mainstays of the side. From Natal.

P. S. HEINE, 26, salesman; 6 ft. 4 in. Tallest member of the side. New to England. Right-hand fast-medium bowler and strong hitter. Brother of Mrs. Bobbie Heine Miller, who used to be one of Wimbledon's leading players. From Orange Free State.

H. J. KEITH, 27, fitter. Left-hander. Another newcomer to England, though he played in Australia in one of the Test Matches—the last—and helped McLean to make the 106 runs needed to give South Africa victory. Bowls spinners. From Natal.

P. N. F. MANSELL, 34, English by birth—his brother plays for the Ealing Club now. An allrounder whose leg-spin bowling has become subservient to his batting. Toured England in 1951 and Australia in 1952–3. Clerk. From Rhodesia.

R. A. McLEAN, 24. The most attractive bat in the side, though there is often a lot of daylight between legs and bat. Played in three Tests in England in 1951 and in five in Australia in 1952–3. His 81 in the fifth brought victory to his country and squared the rubber. Hits the ball harder and more frequently than most. Fine outfield; fly-half at rugby; good golfer and hockey player. From Natal.

A. R. A. MURRAY, 33. All-rounder. First visit to England, but batted and bowled in the Test series in Australia with modest success. Schoolmaster. From Eastern Province.

V. I. SMITH, 29. Played in England in the 1947 side, but missed the 1951 tour. Not chosen for Australia. Learned to bowl his leg-spinners faster and so regained place in international side. From Natal.

H. J. TAYFIELD, 26. Came to England in 1951 late in tour as a reinforcement. In Australia took 30 wickets in five Tests—equal to a record by a visitor there. In 17 Tests against all countries took 78 wickets before recent tour began. Possesses a habit, rather irritating after a while, of stubbing the ground frequently with his right big toe. One of the world's three or four leading off-breakers. From Natal.

J. H. B. WAITE, 25. Batsman-wicketkeeper who visited England in 1951 and Australia in 1952–3. World Test record at home against New Zealand in 1953–4 for greatest number of wickets, 23, in five-match series. Tall, active, spectacular taker of catches. From Transvaal. Stock Exchange.

P. L. WINSLOW, 25. Hitter of the side who early in tour took 30 runs in an over off Jack Ikin of Lancashire. As a colt spent a season under Patsy Hendren as member of the Sussex Club and Ground Staff. Sportsmaster. From Transvaal.

The ages mentioned are those at the beginning of the tour. Several of the players had birthdays in England.

The manager was Ken Viljoen, himself one of the best batsmen ever produced by South Africa. Managed the side in Australia. He scored two centuries in Test cricket—at Manchester 1935 and Melbourne 1931.

Although the South Africans had flown to England, the Union Castle Steamship Company apparently bore them no ill-will, for the "pipe opener" game of the tour—at Blackheath on 4th May—was against the Sports Club of that Line. A twelve-a-side match was won by the South Africans, even though several of their number, including their highest scorers, went into the opposition camp for one day only.

Then, after the usual round of welcomes and feastings, including the dinner given annually by the Cricket Writers' Club to all touring sides, the South Africans passed on to Worcester.

Why, for year after year, this fair towered city should be the scene of the opening match for touring elevens I cannot say. But so it is, and nothing except the weather is likely to alter the arrangement. This time it might have been worse.

Worcestershire, though not nowadays threatening to displace Surrey at the top of the County table, are yet strong

enough to play a good match against even powerful sides new
to English conditions. So it was that the South Africans were
beaten by 117 runs with 65 minutes to spare.

Reg Perks, now at 43 captain of the County, told me he
had been opening the bowling for Worcestershire against touring sides ever since 1931. But his most spectacular performance
in this match was a display of hard hitting at number 10 in the
batting order. His 41 helped to give the first innings total a
respectable appearance at 260. Much earlier in the innings
Kenyon, Outschoorn and Dews had laid a good foundation.

Perks's only wicket in the match was a noteworthy one.
He had the opener, McGlew, l.b.w. before he had scored. The
most successful bowler in the South African first innings was
little Bob Berry from Lancashire, playing in his first match for
his new County. His five for 60 meant that the County had a
first innings lead of 51.

Tayfield, who had taken half the County wickets in the
first innings, repeated the feat in the second. Even so,
Worcestershire, helped by good innings from Dews and
Whitehead, were able to set the South Africans the task of
making 261 to win. They were all out for 143.

This was very much the day of young Martin Horton, now
becoming a regular member of the side. His nine for 56 on a
rain-affected wicket made the England selectors take a first
glance in his direction.

I cannot leave Worcester without recalling a story about
one of the more ornate writers among my professional brethren.
Something went wrong with his "background" description of
the scenery, and his sports editor received the following
correction by telephone:

"For red cathedral read grey cathedral; for muddy
Avon read brown Severn."

That, received on edition time, tends to upset the harmony
of any newspaper office.

After this Worcester reverse the South Africans ran right
into our truly terrible May weather. The next three matches—
at Derby, Nottingham and Cambridge—were all drawn. The

third day at the first two places was a blank. The visitors had the worse of the Derby draw and might well have been beaten, chiefly through the bowling of the three redoubtables, Jackson, Gladwin and Morgan. They finished the first innings ahead of Notts and would almost certainly have beaten Cambridge by an innings had there been time.

The first victory of the tour, appropriately enough, was at Lord's, where a strong M.C.C. side was soundly beaten by 93 runs. Chief influence here was the 87 total which was all the M.C.C. could muster in the first innings. Hutton had to retire ill—the beginning of the trouble which afflicted him more or less throughout the season. He contributed only two runs in the match.

McLean's 85 in the South African second innings was a superb display of stroke-making. The result was highly encouraging, for even with Hutton idle we had international cricketers such as Graveney, Compton, Close, Parks, Bailey, Andrew and Loader in the home side, in addition to Barrington and Titmus who were capped for England soon afterwards. Apart from McLean, no member of the winning team was specially conspicuous; it was an excellent combined operation.

Victory at Lord's was followed immediately by victory at Oxford. Here Goddard scored the first century of the tour; McGlew, most consistent of the batsmen, joined him in an opening three-figure stand and McLean played another good innings. All of which, with other items, added up to 434 for eight declared. Oxford made 90 and 207, with 40 by Fellows-Smith, the highest contribution in either innings.

Again bowling honours were shared, but the starting of the rot in the first innings was due to Goddard and Heine—Heine took five of the first six wickets for 31.

Victory by an innings and 137, coming immediately after the win at Lord's, made the South Africans feel that they were not destined to failure after all.

There followed another wet wicket game at Cardiff, limited by rain to the second and third days. McGlew came along with another of his half-centuries; Fuller produced his best bowling figures yet, but the touring side were 78 behind on the first innings of a drawn game.

I did not see this match, but I did see the following one at Colchester, where, in the middle of the railway strike, our visitors arrived by coach from Cardiff at three in the morning. Happily for them they won the toss on a dry wicket and completely mastered the Essex attack. There were centuries by McGlew and McLean and near-centuries by Mansell and Keith. At the declaration at 503 for four the County bowling figures were of the "nought (or one) for plenty" order. Look at the analysis at the end of this book. I will not drag it further into the light.

A total of 354 by Essex would have saved the follow-on. The County batsmen fell just four short of it, Jack Bailey, the last man, falling after making one good hit and leaving Ken Preston stranded for four not out. This was hard lines after Trevor Bailey and Douglas Insole had each taken a century— the first to be scored off the touring bowlers.

The match was saved, for what that achievement was worth.

The same two batsmen were together again in the second innings when the match ended with Essex hopelessly behind at 89 for five.

Adcock, who had suffered strains in the cold first month of the season and who had missed four out of the first six matches, bowled flat out at Colchester with moderate success. In this high-scoring game the infrequent wickets were well divided by the bowlers of both sides.

The last match before the first Test was at Manchester, and here another blank day—the third allotted to the fixture —was added to the others. The South Africans fell behind on the first innings—154 to 201—but compensated in the second for their lapse. Their 232 for four would probably have enabled them to win.

This match, played at the beginning of June, was the last before the Nottingham Test. Two victories had been won, one game lost and of the six draws only one, that at Derby, went heavily against them—Derby 179 and 100 for four, the South Africans 113.

Thus far in the tour McGlew had proved himself beyond measure the most dependable batsman. Cheetham had played some stubborn innings in times of crisis. Endean, while very far from failing, had not yet lived up to his achievements in Australia. Goddard had begun to establish himself as the side's chief all-rounder. McLean had begun badly but had played several brilliant innings. Waite had kept wicket well and had made several sizable scores.

Winslow had burst in on us every now and then with a piece of hitting, chief of these efforts being the 40 in eight balls against Ikin and Goodwin of Lancashire. Of the bowlers, the off-spinner Tayfield, as expected in such weather conditions, was far ahead of the rest of the field as a wicket-taker. Smith looked a much improved leg-break bowler; Heine and Fuller were running a close race for selection in the side. Adcock, for reasons already mentioned, had not yet run into full form.

Now let me turn to the Englishmen for awhile. Were we to be stronger than in Australia, or the reverse?

CHAPTER III

LEN HUTTON OUT

BEFORE any Test side is selected there comes the selection of the selectors—a statement highly charged with sibilants, but never mind. The committee which had chosen the side to win the Ashes in Australia ought, on the face of it, to have been capable of choosing one to beat South Africa at home. But it did not continue in office.

The selectors for the home series against Pakistan in 1954 were: H. S. Altham (chairman), N. W. D. Yardley, R. W. V. Robins and L. E. G. Ames. When the Australian tour approached G. O. Allen and C. Palmer were added and L. Hutton was co-opted as captain-designate.

Mr. Altham, a retired housemaster at Winchester School, who is hon. treasurer of M.C.C. and mainspring of the national youth coaching scheme, gave up in 1955 the burden of selection, with its constant need of long-distance travel. Others stood down, too, and the selectors for the Tests against South Africa became:

G. O. Allen (chairman), L. E. G. Ames, A. B. Sellers and W. Wooller.

Allen, oddly enough, was serving for the first time as a selector, although as a former captain of England he must have had a hand in the choosing of sides for overseas. Wooller, captain of Glamorgan, was also new; but Sellers, former captain of Yorkshire, now returning to national cricket administration after a period of retirement, had served more than once on selection committees.

One of the first actions of the new committee was to appoint Hutton as captain for the whole series against South Africa and co-opt him as a selector. Now with the principle of choosing a captain for all five Tests I am in whole-hearted agreement. On him is bestowed a prestige he would not have if he were picked "on appro", on a match-by-match basis.

Assuming that his powers as player and leader are proved beyond doubt then this is the only sensible course.

Yet the decision in the case of Hutton proved unfortunate, not because Hutton was an unworthy choice, but because of a breakdown of health and form with the bat.

The strain of captaincy in Australia had asserted itself in a series of low scores in the later Test matches there. But everyone thought that the rest afforded by the long voyage home would renew his energies. Under that assumption Allen and his committee broke recent precedent by making Hutton captain of England for the season.

His breakdown during the South African match against M.C.C. at Lord's was an indication that health trouble was brewing. Fibrositis caused him to retire ill after scoring only two runs in the first innings. He could take no further part in the match. The aches and pains did not subside at once and before the first Test it was announced that Hutton could not stand the strain of a five-day match. The captaincy for that game was handed over to P. B. H. May. In the hope that exercise of a less severe sort would remedy matters Hutton continued to play for Yorkshire, but before the second Test Match it was stated that he had asked to be relieved of Test Match play for the rest of the series. May was confirmed in the leadership for the remaining fixtures.

After that Hutton played for Yorkshire at Nottingham, his first big innings of the season. The question arose whether his decision would be irrevocable. His decision, I was assured, had not been forced upon him by the selectors, who would have held the question open again until the third Test Match.

The Nottingham century was followed by nought and two against Hampshire at Bournemouth, where I asked Hutton direct whether he might come back into the 1955 series. His reply was that he was still not fit for long Test Matches and it would not be fair to keep some other player out. The Bournemouth match was followed by another enforced rest, even from the County game.

Hutton told me how bitterly he felt the disappointment, if only for the personal reason that he wanted to captain England in more Tests than the record set up by W. M. Woodfull for

Australia. Hutton, since his appointment as captain in 1952—the first professional leader since the very old days when tours were commercial propositions—had led his country in four matches against India, ten against Australia, five against West Indies, and two each against Pakistan and New Zealand, a total of 23, the highest achieved by an Englishman. Woodfull captained Australia 25 times.

Hutton was 39 years of age on 23rd June, when he might have been playing in the Test Match at Lord's. Have we seen the last of him in the England side? I devoutly hope not. We have to play the Australians in England next year. At the moment of writing this chapter the problem of England's opening pair has certainly not been solved.

As long as Hutton was fit and in form half this problem was perpetually settled; now this is so no longer. Hobbs-Rhodes, Hobbs-Sutcliffe, Hutton-Washbrook—where are their successors now? I mean the men who can not only set the England innings going handsomely once now and then, but can do it as a matter of habit. When two men like that are found then we can afford to let Hutton go into retirement.

A winter's rest may well make Hutton fit again. The trouble is due as much to nerve-strain as to purely physical causes, and freedom for seven months from cricket should restore him.

That does not mean that Hutton will captain England again, for now another man is in the saddle. I do not think Hutton's reappointment to anything more than the highly important post of England's number one batsman would be desirable. He has borne well the burden of leadership in half a dozen different campaigns. Let him concentrate now on making runs again.

Hutton, than whom I have never had a better friend in cricket, remarked to me that making "all those runs" was telling its tale on him. I looked him up in the carefully compiled Career Records of Roy Webber in the *Playfair Cricket Annual*. They number 38,354 in his career, excluding the last Australian-New Zealand tour and excluding also his scores this year. Hutton himself calculated that 27,000 to 28,000 had been made since the war.

At the beginning of the 1955 season his centuries numbered

128, two more than those of the immortal W. G. Grace—but remember that in W. G.'s day overseas tour were few. Above Hutton in the list of centurions, compiled by *Wisden*, are Hobbs, top of them all with 197, Hendren 170, Hammond 167, Mead 153, Sutcliffe 149 and Woolley 145. I fear that to lead this list will be beyond Hutton's accomplishment, but the honour of making top score in Test cricket—364 against Australia at the Oval in 1938—is likely to remain his for good. I trust so, for 13-hour innings even by a Len Hutton are apt to become boring after the seventh or eighth hour.

I have drifted too much into cricket history. There is no need yet to regard Hutton as a back number. Jack—I ought to write "Sir John"—Hobbs made some thousands of runs after the age of forty. Hutton may do the same.

The fifteen Englishmen who played in one or more Test Matches in Australia last winter were, to name them in any order, L. Hutton, P. B. H. May, T. W. Graveney, D. C. S. Compton, T. E. Bailey, M. C. Cowdrey, W. J. Edrich, R. Appleyard, J. H. Wardle, T. G. Evans, J. B. Statham, F. H. Tyson, R. T. Simpson, A. V. Bedser and K. V. Andrew. The side which clinched the Ashes in the fourth Test at Adelaide were these fifteen less Simpson, Graveney, Bedser and Andrew.

Everyone home from Australia was available for the first Test Match against the South Africans with two exceptions—Hutton and Cowdrey, the one for reasons already elaborated, the other because of the calls of National Service. Cowdrey had disappeared from public view to do his "square bashing" in the R.A.F. up at Hednesford, in Staffordshire. For the time being he was having no cricket at all and could not be considered for the England side.

Between the first and second Tests Cowdrey became a civilian again. The R.A.F. doctors had decided that some old-standing foot trouble made him unsuitable for service. And that was that. While Cowdrey, thus surprisingly restored to freedom to play cricket, was doing so at Lord's, his case was being discussed in the Commons—a coincidence without precedent for a cricketer.

I am in no position to discuss the rights and wrongs of the Cowdrey case and have no desire to do so. Like many thousands

Members of the 1955 South African Cricket Team. (*Back row, left to right*): C. Duckworth (Rhodesia), L. Smith (Natal), P. Winslow (Transvaal), P. Heine (Orange Free State), N. Adcock (Transvaal), T. Goddard (Natal), H. Keith (Natal) and E. Fuller (Western Province). (*Front row, left to right*): R. McLean (Natal), J. Waite (Transvaal), W. R. Endean (Transvaal), J. Cheetham (Western Province, capt.), J. McGlew (Natal, vice-capt.), P. Mansell (Rhodesia), A. Tayfield (Natal) and A. Murray (Eastern Province)

H.M. THE QUEEN shaking hands with the visitors on the Oval Ground

Peter May and Jack Cheetham, the rival captains, toss at Trent Bridge. May won and decided that England should bat first

FIRST
TEST

England's new opening pair, Kenyon (*left*) and Graveney, take the field to bat against South Africa

of others I wondered at the time why, since Cowdrey was unfit, he was taken into the R.A.F. at all—a waste of his own
time and the nation's money. But that apart, let me make this
clear—that Colin Cowdrey is the last man in the world of
cricket to attempt, or be party to, a "wangle" for his own
benefit. He merely submitted to the divinity which shapes our
ends. It was all he—or we—can do.

May I add this too—that the fact that Cowdrey made
centuries at cricket immediately after his discharge as unfit for
service is no proof that the trouble had miraculously passed
away. In fact it has not. The stiffening of the foot which afflicts
him is a gradual matter.

Sooner or later, he tells me, an operation will be necessary.
He is trying to delay the evil hour as long as possible, for it may
not achieve a permanent cure.

Meanwhile everyone welcomes him back to cricket.

The chairman of selectors, G. O. Allen, has a happy way
of dealing with newspapermen. He invites cricket corres-
pondents to a conference at Lord's immediately after the side
is chosen, announces the eleven names, gives out any accompany-
ing official statement, and then has an "off the record" chat
containing much background information. A writer can know
what is in the selectors' minds. Here is a much better plan than
that of years ago, when the names were merely telephoned
to a news agency without any why or wherefore or other
supplementary information.

Back in 1936-7, when Allen captained the English side in
Australia, I found the same readiness on his part to give the
why and the wherefore to responsible journalists. And why
not? Cricket is a game, not an exercise in high diplomacy.
There was a time when Lord's was as secretive as the Foreign
Office. Sometimes it is so now.

When, before the opening of the Nottingham Test Match,
the England side became known it contained eight of the
eleven who had won the Adelaide Test. Omitted were Hutton,
W. A. Edrich and Cowdrey. In their places were D. J. Kenyon,
T. W. Graveney (who played in two Tests in Australia but not
the "Ashes" one) and K. Barrington of Surrey, the only newcomer to Test cricket—he had only recently been given his

County cap. G. A. R. Lock was named among twelve, but was omitted from the side on the morning of the match.

There were many, including myself, who would have played Lock rather than Wardle. A. V. Bedser, W. Watson and one or two others had their advocates, but on the whole it was agreed that the selectors had done their job well.

What of the South Africans? All through the tour they showed a strange reluctance to announce their side until the morning of a match. This was understandable in doubtful weather when the question of playing fast or spin bowlers might arise, but later, on the eve of the third Test in settled weather, they still confined their announcement to a panel of thirteen. One incidental result of this was confusion next day over the score-card, whose early edition had to go to Press with a South African side of thirteen.

It was not until tossing-time that we knew which eleven would play. Then they were named as follows: J. E. Cheetham, D. J. McGlew, T. L. Goddard, J. H. Waite, W. R. Endean, R. A. McLean, P. L. Winslow, H. J. Tayfield, E. R. H. Fuller, V. I. Smith and N. A. T. Adcock.

Omitted were C. A. R. Duckworth, the reserve wicket-keeper, P. S. Heine, fast-medium bowler, H. J. Keith, left-hand bat and slow left-hand bowler, P. N. F. Mansell, batsman and leg-spin bowler, and A. R. A. Murray, fast-medium bowler and batsman.

CHAPTER IV

THE FIRST TEST MATCH

*Played at Nottingham, 9th, 10th, 11th, 13th, 14th June,
and won by England at 5.15 on the fourth day by an
innings and five runs.*

WHATEVER may be said in criticism of the slowness of
the wicket at Trent Bridge—and such revilings are frequent—Nottingham remains my favourite English provincial
Test Match ground. Indeed, even the word "provincial" might
be omitted. Trent Bridge has tradition and it has modernity.
The ground itself is pleasant—still a field rather than a stadium,
Nottingham and its castle and river always have strong appeal; the score-board, on the Australian pattern, betokens a
progressive County committee, and the Press box, until the
new one at Leeds became its close rival, stood out as the best
in the country.

To anyone who, like myself, reports Test Matches for an
evening paper, nearness to a telephone comes next in import-
ance to a good view of the game. In this matter Lord's, which
ought to be first among English Test grounds, comes a bad
last. The poor telephonist has to run up and down that steep,
two-decker outdoor staircase a dozen or more times a day and
then push through the crowd to his telephone-box fifty yards
away. Nottingham, Manchester, the Oval and Leeds all set an
example in this respect.

Birmingham, as the second city in England, has long been
pleading for Test Matches, and now is to have them, largely
at the expense of Nottingham, partly at the expense of the two
Northern grounds. The justice of the Warwickshire claim cannot be denied; the pity of it is that there are only five Test
Matches to distribute. Next year, however, the first Text Match
against Australia will again be on Trent-side.

This first Test of 1955 proved to be one of the dreariest I
have ever seen. In the three and a half days' cricket which

began and ended the match only 663 runs were scored—a miserable output which was not explained by the bowling until the last-day performance of Frank Tyson. His six wickets for 28 compared on paper, if hardly in actual fact, with his seven for 27 in the Melbourne Test some months before.

Here is the day-by-day progress of the match.

FIRST DAY

England, winning the toss, scored 244 for four wickets in the six hours' play.

Here on this opening day was no great display of stroke-making batting to compensate for the cold wind which extended the flags over the pavilion and drove into overcoats the crowd of about 10,000 on this unseasonable June day. The best that could be said was that England had made a fair start in a dour and grim manner matching the weather.

Kenyon, restored to Test cricket because of his fine County record for Worcestershire, opened the innings with Graveney and for once an English first pair gave the side a really good start. The two West Countrymen put on 91 before Graveney was out.

The South African attack was launched by Adcock, undeniably fast, and Goddard, medium-pace left-hand. Goddard, by the way, opened the South African batting next day too—a rare distinction for which Trevor Bailey in the West Indies can furnish a precedent. Against these two bowlers the Englishmen had only one adventure before lunch. When he had scored two Kenyon played a hard ball from Adcock to Tayfield close in at silly mid-on. The only result was a tingling of fingers for the fieldsman; the chance was missed.

Graveney had his luck without giving a positive chance. The first of his four boundaries before lunch was an edger through the slips which might have gone anywhere but was debited as four runs against Adcock. There would probably have been a fifth four to Graveney, but for a heap of unused sawdust, placed precautionarily by the groundsman behind wicket. It acted as a bunker. Before lunch the seam bowling of Adcock, Goddard and Fuller was reinforced by the spinners of

Tayfield, but by the break 79 rather unspectacular runs had been scored—Kenyon 41, Graveney 35.

After lunch the partnership was ended when it had existed for 2¼ hours. Graveney reached forward to a ball which may have moved away from him, and a catch behind the stumps gave Adcock his first Test wicket in England. One for 92. By now Smith, the last of the five regular bowlers in the side, was having his first bowl of the day.

Kenyon and May took the total from 91 to 166 before Kenyon was out. During their stand the 100 total was passed. Kenyon approached—without reaching—his century. It was nearly tea-time when he was l.b.w. in trying to hit to leg a ball from Goddard. One sympathised with him in falling 13 short of his hundred in a Test career of moderate success.

When Kenyon left Compton stayed with May in a stand of 64 which would have been of greater value but for the agility of half a dozen off-side fieldsmen—a sort of mobile human wall—whom the batsmen tried to elude in vain. Time after time they hammered balls from Smith and Goddard into the covers, with everything they had got behind the stroke; hardly ever did the ball pass through. The new ball, taken belatedly, ended Compton's innings with a catch at the wicket off Adcock. Two hundred and twenty-eight for three.

Barrington merely came and went, making, as Hutton did long ago, a duck in his first Test Match. The ball from Fuller lifted awkwardly and again Waite had a catch, this time off the bowling of Fuller. Two hundred and thirty-three for four.

Enter Bailey to hold on to the end in this semi-crisis. That last half-hour had cost us two wickets, but May was still there for 81 after 3¾ hours. A day of little liveliness and moderate achievement.

SECOND DAY

England's score was advanced from 244 for four to a total of 334. South Africa at close of play had made 83 for five wickets.

Nine solid hours did it take the cream of England's batsmen, with Hutton an all-important absentee, to accumulate their total of 334. It was a moderate score and at one time we looked like making 100 runs more. Not once or twice in our rough island story Trevor Bailey's path of duty was the way to glory. Inconspicuous glory perhaps, for the 49 runs which this last-ditcher made took three hours and a quarter to collect; but we should have been in a sorry way without him.

May, who had scored 81 overnight, added only two before his departure. Bowling to him and Bailey was a combination of slow-medium leg-spin from Smith and fast stuff from Adcock. There seemed no reason why another crisis should develop, but develop it did. Bailey, who the previous night had scored only a single, hooked for four a long hop from Smith. But with the day only ten minutes old May was out. He received a ball rather similar to the one Bailey had hit, but not quite so short. In trying to hit it over the head of mid-wicket for a boundary he sent it "down the throat" of McGlew. He had batted nearly all the previous afternoon and evening, and his 83 contained five fours.

In came Godfrey Evans, playing a very un-Evans-like innings of an hour and a quarter. He and Bailey put on 33, of which Evans scored only 12. He was 20 minutes making his first single, and, very unusually, received a round of ironical applause for the feat. Later we did have a sample or two of Evans's liveliness. He twice ran out and drove Tayfield for four, and once, in running a single for his partner, completed the journey sliding full-length on his undercarriage.

Goddard, most economical of the South African bowlers, sent down ten overs for seven maidens and nine runs. Then Fuller, who bowls a lively medium-pace, succeeded him and had Evans caught by Goddard in the gully. Two hundred and eighty-five for six.

Wardle, whom crowds always expect to hit the cover off the ball, was as quiet as Evans for fifteen minutes. Then he tried his favourite "cow shot", missed, started to run a leg-bye but was pulled up by the umpire's decision that he was out l.b.w. Two hundred and ninety-four for seven.

Tyson did not score. With the total 298 he tried a grand slam which would have made it 300 but hoisted a catch. And so to lunch.

In the early afternoon Statham became the most effective of the tail-enders. He made attacking strokes against Tayfield and Fuller while Bailey went on in his own unruffled way. Statham, after contributing 20 towards a stand of 36 with Bailey, was caught at the wicket off Fuller. Three hundred and thirty-four for nine.

Appleyard the last man played one ball, and then Bailey, still one short of his half-century, was l.b.w. to Goddard.

England were all out for 334, which on this quiet wicket did not seem a total which could achieve a follow-on. But in cricket all things are possible.

Fifty minutes before tea-time the South African innings began. From then until the end of the day that courageous little batsman McGlew held up his side's innings. Five wickets went down for 83 and he was undefeated at the end for 38.

Statham and Tyson opened the bowling together—the finest new-ball attack in the world with the still possible exception of Lindwall and Miller. The very first ball bowled by Tyson entered Evans's glove almost before Goddard realised it was on the way. Even so, McGlew and Goddard kept their wickets intact until it looked as though the edge was wearing off the fast bowlers. But at that point Goddard was l.b.w. to Statham. Fifteen for one.

Two runs later Waite was run out by a fine throw from Statham at deep third man. Waite was trying for a third run for his partner when this happened. Statham in the outfield, or indeed anywhere else, is one of the fieldsman with whom no batsman should take risks. His throwing is up to the best Australian standards. Endean, batting in a poor light, was soon l.b.w. to Tyson, and three men were out for 19.

After tea McLean figured in a 16-runs stand with McGlew before Tyson bowled him. Thirty-five for four.

Winslow restrained himself awhile, but then gave a catch at mid-on in trying to hit Appleyard. Fifty-five for five. Cheetham played out time with McGlew and indeed added some useful runs.

THIRD DAY

South Africa, all out 181, failed by four runs to avoid
the follow-on. The English captain enforced it, and
South Africa in their second innings scored 46 for no
wickets.

Early in the day it certainly did not appear that Peter May
would be able to ask his opponents to bat again. McGlew (68)
and Cheetham (54) completed a stand of 94. But the South
African tail failed to wag.

Immediately play began the two wreckers of the previous
night, Tyson and Statham, were turned on by their captain.
This time they had no success. McGlew, 38 overnight, and
Cheetham, 17, re-entered the field with the position of their
side as bleak as the weather, which grew colder and gloomier
all morning.

Tyson bowled for half an hour, Statham for an hour in their
first spell. They were not expensive, but could not disturb the
batsmen.

Appleyard and Wardle succeeded them and their success
was considerably delayed. Slow the cricket was, but we English
had no right to criticise. McGlew and Cheetham scored less
slowly than had our batsmen before lunch the previous day.
They made 57, we only 54 during the morning, and the time
of the South Africans was a quarter of an hour less because the
umpires stopped play during bad light.

During the interval some dozens of Nottingham boy
cricketers went on to the field, sweaterless in the bitter cold
and gloom, and gave a mass coaching demonstration under
their instructors. Here was a fine exhibition of young cricket
enthusiasm.

The light had improved, though the sky was still overcast when play was resumed. Cheetham with his first single
passed his previous best score of the tour—35 against Lancashire.

Wardle was bowling with Tyson, maiden over after
maiden over. At the beginning of his eleventh runless over
McGlew tried a cut and was caught behind the wicket.

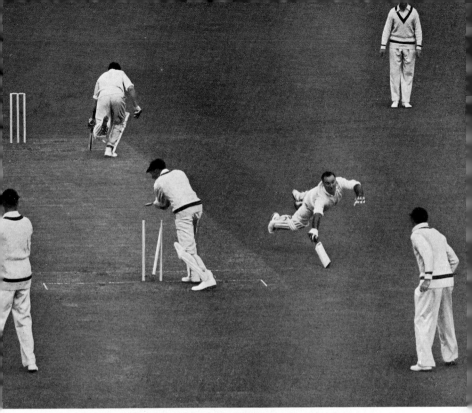

Evans only just scrambles home with a spectacular leap
as Waite tries to run him out

FIRST TEST

Tyson bowling to South African opener, McGlew, on the second day

(*Top*) : Tayfield out, caught by Bailey during the third day's play at Trent Bridge

(*Centre*) : Tayfield had just previously narrowly escaped being run out, by this smart return from Barrington

(*Below*) : McGlew places one nicely between two England players for 4

Wardle's figures at that moment were extraordinary: 19·1—
14—15—1. The stand had realised 94 in rather over three
hours, but McGlew had been in for just over five. One hundred
and forty-nine for six and 36 needed to save the follow-on.

Tayfield joined Cheetham, whose seventh boundary took
his score past 50. Wardle went on bowling runless overs. Tayfield scored a single off him to short leg—a run which was
fatal to Cheetham. Facing Wardle, he was caught by Graveney
at first slip. Wardle's figures since lunch now read: 8—7—1—2.
One hundred and fifty-six for seven, or 29 now required.

Tayfield and Fuller looked like saving the follow-on when
they took the score to 174 with the aid of some luck. Only
11 were now needed, but only 7 were obtained. Tayfield was
caught in the slips by Bailey off Appleyard—174 for eight.
Fuller, without reverence, hit Wardle for a six, and now only
five were necessary. Fuller tried to repeat the six hit but missed
and was bowled, and when the last man, Adcock, came in, five
more runs were required. He made one of them, but his partner
Smith, after declining to hit a slow full-pitch from Wardle to
the place where it should have gone, put up an easy catch to
May close to the bat.

There was some doubt whether May would enforce the
follow-on, for this was only the third day of a five-day match
and his bowlers were tiring. He decided to take the risk, and
although no South African wicket fell for the rest of the day
the step he took fully justified itself. At close of play McGlew
and Goddard had made 46 without loss.

Let me quote Wardle's extraordinary figures for the first
innings: 32—23—24—4. From only nine overs in that long
bowling effort had any runs accrued.

FOURTH DAY

*South Africa were all out in their second innings for
148. At 5.15 p.m., a day early, England won by an
innings and five runs.*

Here indeed was a quick result, all the quicker because on
that Monday morning the ground was so wet from the Sunday

rain that cricket was not possible until 1 p.m. Only about 2000 people saw the resumption of the game at a time fixed by the umpires after the two captains had left the decision to them—a polite way of intimating that they were not in agreement. Nottingham had not supported this Test Match as well as it might; slow cricket and the railway strikes were deterrent influences.

On came the English spinners at once to bowl to the overnight not-outs McGlew and Goddard. Wardle went on providing maiden overs, of which 30 already stood to his credit in the match. Four of the six overs he bowled before lunch were runless, and only a single came off each of the other two. A two and a single to McGlew off Appleyard, and a four in byes made up the sum total of the runs in the brief morning play.

Then came the inflexible lunch break. This meal is like the law of the Medes and Persians—it altereth not in Test Matches. A little give and take in the regulations would have enabled the players to have their food while the ground was drying. In matches between the South Africans and Counties the lunch intervals may be varied, just as the tea break often is. In Test Matches lunch is from 1.30 p.m. to 2.10 p.m. and no power on earth can change it.

After lunch Goddard at last added three runs to his overnight 21—a hit to leg off Appleyard. He scored another run presently from Wardle—a cannon off Barrington's shin-bone which took a knock as its owner stood behind the bat. There followed two boundaries, one by Goddard off Wardle, the other by McGlew off Appleyard.

Things were not going well with us. The chances of a fourth-day innings victory looked forlorn. Tyson replaced Appleyard at 73.

What the bowlers could not do a run-out achieved. McGlew played a ball hard to Statham at mid-wicket and his partner backed up. Statham returned the ball smartly to the bowler, Wardle, who stuck out his foot. The ball rebounded from the sole of his boot to the stumps. It looked to me as though Goddard would not have been out if he had grounded his bat a second or two sooner.

This opening partnership had been worth 73 runs to the South Africans. The next one, between McGlew and Waite, was worth only 10. Waite, after ducking a couple of bumpers from Tyson, received a ball bowled to a length which rose smartly. It hit the bat high on the blade and was spooned into the air to Compton in the leg-trap.

In came Endean and off went Wardle, who had bowled that day 13 overs, 8 of them maidens, for 14 runs. McGlew completed his half-century off Appleyard, which had taken him nearly four hours. It was his second of the match.

Next Bailey, Tyson's relief, had his first wicket in either innings when Endean snicked a catch to Graveney at first slip. One hundred and one for three; 52 now needed to make England bat again.

Not long afterwards Bailey took a second and more valuable wicket. McGlew, after scoring 51, received a sharp riser which he lifted to May for a catch in the slips. One hundred and eight for four.

By now prospects were black indeed for the South Africans. McLean and Cheetham, in a stand of 23, raised their hopes again of avoiding the innings defeat. A dangerous man this McLean, and no opponent can be sure of victory until his back is turned. Just before tea Tyson had him caught cleverly at second slip, low and to Graveney's right. One hundred and thirty-one for five.

A quick changeover by the English fieldsmen allowed Tyson to get in another over. In it he bowled Cheetham. One hundred and thirty-two for six.

After tea it was merely a matter of time—and not much time at that. Tayfield was bowled by the all-conquering Tyson with the score unchanged. Winslow, as usual, tried to hit, but was bowled, too. For a change Fuller was caught off Wardle by Evans. The last pair, Smith and Adcock, delayed the end for twenty minutes before Adcock's middle stump was laid flat. South Africa were all out for 148, and the English victory was complete.

The crowd had increased in the afternoon's sunshine to about 5000. They had a short ration of play, yet had value for money in watching Tyson run through the opposition batsmen.

His analysis that afternoon was six wickets for 11 runs in 13 overs and three balls; his figures for the whole innings were 21·3—7—28—6. Sheer speed and ability to make the good length ball rise sharply on occasions were the factors in his success.

Heavy though their defeat was, one could sympathise with the South Africans because of the long cold wet spell of early summer, continuing even into this first Test Match, so alien to their experience in their homeland. One felt they were capable of much better things, and so we found later, to our cost, in the Third Test at Manchester.

ENGLAND

FIRST INNINGS

D. Kenyon lbw b Goddard	..	..	..	87
T. W. Graveney c Waite b Adcock	..	..	..	42
P. B. H. May c McGlew b Smith	..	..	..	83
D. C. S. Compton lbw b Adcock	..	..	..	27
K. Barrington c Waite b Fuller	..	..	..	0
T. E. Bailey lbw b Goddard	..	..	..	49
T. G. Evans c Goddard b Fuller	..	..	..	12
J. H. Wardle lbw b Tayfield	..	..	..	2
F. H. Tyson c McLean b Tayfield	..	..	..	0
J. B. Statham c Waite b Fuller	..	..	..	20
R. Appleyard not out	..	..	..	0
Extras	..	..	..	12
Total	..	..	..	**334**

FALL OF WICKETS

1—91; 2—166; 3—228; 4—233; 5—252; 6—285; 7—294; 8—298; 9—334.

Peter May, England's
captain, sweeps at a ball
from Goddard

Graveney hits a single
off Adcock (South
Africa)

Statham was well on the
wicket during the second
day's play when he delivered
the last ball before lunch
which rooted out the middle
stump of South Africa's
R. A. McLean

Graveney is well caught by Heine after making 60

Heine again fields well, to stop a Compton "special"

Tayfield is caught by Evans off Statham for
3 during the fourth day's play at Lord's

BOWLING

	O.	M.	R.	W.
Adcock	36	9	74	2
Goddard	36·4	18	61	2
Fuller	29	5	59	3
Tayfield	37	11	66	2
Smith	30	9	62	1

SOUTH AFRICA

FIRST INNINGS

D. J. McGlew c Evans b Wardle	68
T. L. Goddard lbw b Statham	12
J. H. B. Waite run out	0
W. R. Endean lbw b Tyson	0
R. A. McLean b Tyson	13
P. L. Winslow c May b Appleyard	2
J. E. Cheetham c Graveney b Wardle	54
H. J. Tayfield c Bailey b Appleyard	11
E. R. H. Fuller b Wardle	15
V. I. Smith c May b Wardle	0
N. A. T. Adcock not out	1
Extras	5
Total	181

FALL OF WICKETS

1—15; 2—17; 3—19; 4—35; 5—55; 6—149; 7—156; 8—174; 9—180.

BOWLING

	O.	M.	R.	W.
Statham	25	5	47	1
Tyson	24	5	51	2
Bailey	5	2	8	0
Appleyard	28	9	46	2
Wardle	32	23	24	4

D

Second Innings

D. J. McGlew c May b Bailey	.. .. ..	51
T. L. Goddard run out	.. ..	32
J. H. B. Waite c Compton b Tyson	.. ..	3
W. R. Endean c Graveney b Bailey	.. ..	6
R. A. McLean c Graveney b Tyson		16
J. E. Cheetham b Tyson	.. ..	5
P. L. Winslow b Tyson	.. ..	3
H. J. Tayfield b Tyson	.. ..	0
E. R. H. Fuller c Evans b Wardle	.. ..	6
V. I. Smith not out ..	.. ..	2
N. A. T. Adcock b Tyson	.. .. ..	6
Extras ..	.. ..	18
Total	.. ..	148

Fall of Wickets

1—73; 2—83; 3—101; 4—108; 5—131; 6—132; 7—132; 8—135; 9—141.

Bowling

	O.	M.	R.	W.
Statham ..	.. 10	4	16	0
Tyson ..	.. 21·3	7	28	6
Bailey ..	.. 17	8	21	2
Wardle ..	.. 29	17	33	1
Appleyard	.. 19	4	32	0

England won by an innings and 5 runs.

CHAPTER V

APPROACH SHOTS BEFORE LORD'S

TO any cricket tourist the transition from the fever heat of a Test Match to the comparative tranquillity of a game of lesser account is a pleasant contrast. In Australia last winter the English cricketers, after losing the Brisbane Test Match by an innings and 154 runs, found themselves in that land of milk and honey, North Queensland, with Rockhampton and neighbourhood as their opponents. In my own case I managed to do even better that watch cricket. I flew further north to the Great Barrier Reef, but that story has already been told.

The South Africans, after losing at Nottingham, had a long and tiring coach journey south, but it ended in the pleasant county town of Taunton. Whether the two matches-a-week English tours are more strenuous than those in countries with less cricket and more travel is debatable, but they certainly do allow the spare men to keep in practice. At Taunton Keith, Duckworth, Mansell, Murray and Heine, none of whom had played in the first Test Match, had their practice.

South Africa beat Somerset by an innings and 32 runs, even though their own total was no higher than 270 for nine declared. Cheetham, not out 87, and Keith 49, were the top scorers, and Heine reaped a harvest of cheap wickets.

From Taunton to Hove, where Sussex began the match far more resplendently than they finished it. There were centuries from Jim Parks and David Sheppard, making possible a declaration at 352 for six. Sussex seemed to have quite a chance of winning, but McLean contributed a characteristic century in reply, and McGlew, the acting captain, declared when 44 runs behind the County. The Sussex second innings, all out 97, contained no contributions of any consequence, except 45 by Parks.

I watched Fuller's seven for 61 and could not help wondering why he was dropped for the ensuing Test Match. An excellent piece of lively fast-medium bowling it was.

However, dropped he was and so were Winslow and Smith. This in-and-out business in Test Matches is all part of the game. Winslow, who had scored two and three at Nottingham, was to reappear two Tests later at Manchester and hit a wonderful century. Luck plays a dominating part in cricket.

The two changes in the English side were both made necessary by injuries. Appleyard and Tyson had to take a rest, and Titmus, the Middlesex off-break bowler, playing in his first Test, and Trueman, who had not played for England since the tour in the West Indies, filled the vacancies. Titmus had been having a wonderful time in his County side. Indeed, a little later in the season he was one of the three bowlers, the others being Lock and Wardle, who were first to reach their hundred wickets on the same day. His batting was good enough to give him a useful place in the lower middle order, and his fielding was quick and safe, as befitted a keen young man of 22. At the same time the injury to Appleyard was a distinct loss. Trueman had been bowling well for Yorkshire.

The two teams, therefore, were as follows:

England:
    Kenyon, Graveney, May, Compton, Barrington, Bailey, Evans, Titmus, Wardle, Statham, Trueman.

South Africa:
    McGlew, Goddard, Cheetham, Endean, McLean, Waite, Keith, Mansell, Tayfield, Heine, Adcock.
    Such was their order of batting.

CHAPTER VI

THE SECOND TEST MATCH

*Played at Lord's, 23rd, 24th, 25th, 27th, 28th June,
and won by England by 71 runs at 5 p.m. on the fourth
day.*

FIRST DAY

*On the first day England won the toss, batted and were
all out for 133 and South Africa replied with 142 for
five.*

OBVIOUSLY the men who rule in Test Matches at home
had been disturbed by the stodginess of the cricket as
played at Nottingham. If this sort of safety-first batting went
on the gullible public, who flock to Test Matches of whatever
label in the belief that they are going to see something marvell-
ous, would become gullible no longer. The Test Match at
Lord's must be gingered up. So indeed it was.

The wicket, lively and richly grassed, on which the ball
could move and lift, was a credit to Groundsman Swannell.
Though he had been, man and boy, at Lord's for 31 years this
was the first Test Match pitch for which he was responsible
as head groundsman. No doubt he had been encouraged
from the pavilion to provide a pitch with life, and he certainly
succeeded.

Many captains, knowing the dangers of these green
wickets, would just as soon lose the toss as win it, for the
decision to bat, though inevitable, may lead to all sorts of
trouble. A green wicket quietens down when the juice is worn
out of the grass and it becomes easier to bat on the second
day than on the first. On the other hand the disadvantage of
batting last on the fourth or fifth day remains a serious one.
So what would you? What Peter May did was what nine

captains out of ten would have done, he decided to bat, and his side were all out for 133.

For the first 20 minutes of the game there was no hint of the troubles ahead. Then Kenyon, playing defensively to a ball well pitched up to him, helped it into his stumps with the inside of his bat. The score was 7 for one wicket. That wicket was Adcock's, but it was the other fast bowler, Heine, 6 feet 4 ins., and playing in his first Test Match, who broke the back of our innings. May came in, played the remaining ball of Adcock's over, was brought opposite Heine by a single to Graveney and was out for a duck to the last ball of this over. He followed a shortish delivery outwards and touched it to Tayfield at third slip. Eight for two wickets.

It is curious how May has bracketed high scores with low in his Test Matches. In Australia last winter his Test scores were 1 and 44, 5 and 104, 0 and 91, 1 and 26, (one innings only in the Fifth Test) 79. It follows that any bowler who gets May out for a duck in the first innings must look out for trouble in the second. One sympathised with May in failing on his first appearance at Lord's as England's captain.

These two quick casualties had come as a surprise. Kenyon and Graveney, who had put on 91 together at Nottingham, had opened solidly enough together—until Kenyon was out. Compton succeeded May and produced as his first stroke of any account an off-drive for three off Adcock. Heine was given his first rest after 40 minutes' bowling with the total 18. Goddard replaced him and appealed for l.b.w. against Compton. Umpire Laurie Gray, in saying "not out", gave the first decision he had had to make in a Test Match. Soon Heine was brought to the pavilion end to relieve Adcock. Here he had the breeze behind him.

Graveney was next to go. With the total 30 he snicked to Waite a catch off Heine. It was a good ball that got him. So thus early in the innings young Barrington, who had made a duck at Nottingham, had to make a second entry at a highly nervous moment. He scored his first runs with a cover-drive for four off Goddard. McGlew tried a sort of soccer goalkeeper save at full length, but the ball cannoned off his hands and sped on to the ropes.

Compton and Barrington added 15 runs together before Compton received a ball which rose abruptly, struck the shoulder of the bat, and passed thence to Keith in the gully for an easy catch. This ball might have got anyone, so high and unexpected was the hop. Now Heine in his first bowl in a Test Match had taken three for 23 in ten overs.

Already Bailey, although lunch was still three-quarters of an hour away, was needed as the saviour of the side. He hit Heine for the four which brought up the 50, but he had a hazardous time when facing that bowler. Barrington had a let-off in snicking a ball from Heine hard through the slips between Goddard and Mansell. The fieldsmen got in each other's way in diving for the catch.

How Bailey and Barrington stayed together for that three-quarters of an hour I do not know, but stay they did. Ten minutes before lunch Heine came off after bowling during the morning 15 overs for 38 runs and three wickets.

After lunch Heine resumed his attack, bowling in company with Goddard. Off each of them Barrington hit a nice boundary, an on-drive and an off-drive. This was no bad effort by this Surrey lad in a crisis. But with the score 82 Bailey had to go. He stretched right forward to Goddard and was given out l.b.w. Bailey had stayed for an hour for 13 and he and Barrington had added 37.

Evans had an adventurous innings. He lifted a ball, only just out of the reach of long leg's upstretched arms, to the boundary, and the total entered the nineties. At 98 Barrington hit round a ball from Heine in trying to drive him and was bowled. He had batted 95 minutes for 34, including five fours.

Evans, now joined by Titmus, was assisted by an overthrow for four in taking the total past the hundred. He had made 20 when he flirted with a ball over his off-stump and was caught at the wicket. One hundred and eleven for seven and Heine now five for 54.

Three wickets fell at this same total. Titmus, after scoring four in his first Test innings was l.b.w., and Statham was caught at cover off a skier. Wardle, now in with the last man Trueman, delighted himself and everyone else by hitting two successive balls from Goddard for six each—mighty "mow" shots into the crowd in the Mound Stand. He continued to lay about him until he had made 20 in five strokes—two sixes, a four, a three and a single. Then he lifted the inevitable catch to Tayfield at cover, and the innings ended for 133 nearly an hour before tea.

Heine ought to have been presented with the ball he had used so well in his first Test innings. With it he had taken five wickets for 60 runs in 25 overs.

By close of play the South Africans were nine runs ahead with five wickets in hand. Their innings began even worse than ours. The very first ball bowled by Statham got a wicket, McGlew being caught by Evans.

There followed an astonishing opening over from Trueman. He let the first ball slip without delivering it, bowled a no-ball, gave away four byes that were almost wides and then had Goddard caught by a piece of acrobatics by Evans such as only he among wicketkeepers can produce. Goddard glanced the ball with sure touch, but Evans was over there in a flash. Seven for two wickets.

Endean and Cheetham—the latter had put himself in unusually early in the crisis—pulled things together for their side. They put on 44 in company. Cheetham might have been caught by Evans off Trueman when only two; the chance was much less difficult than the one he had taken. Endean when nine was missed by Wardle at short leg. After a stand lasting more than an hour Cheetham was l.b.w. to Bailey.

There followed another stand worth 50 between Endean and McLean which ensured a lead for South Africa. McLean, as usual, scored faster than his partner, taking boundaries off Trueman, Bailey and Wardle. At 101 Endean was l.b.w. to Wardle.

McLean, during a brief partnership with Waite, hooked Statham for six. Waite at 138 became the third victim of Evans and the second of Trueman, and the day ended with McLean still in command with 62 and Keith not out, but runless.

SECOND DAY

South Africa were all out for 304—a lead of 171.
England in the second innings made 108 for one.

By comparison with the previous day the wicket was tame, but again our start was a bad one. When May led his men out Statham and Trueman were turned loose against McLean and Keith. The first of several mistakes in the field came when Bailey did not take a difficult chance given by McLean off Statham to second slip. McLean scored a single instead of losing a wicket.

From the other end, with back to the nursery, Trueman bowled with his air of jaunty aggression. The first boundary of the day, hit by McLean to square leg off Trueman, brought the batsman his highest score thus far against England. His previous best was 67 at Leeds in 1951.

McLean was missed again when he was 80. Facing Statham he cut a ball hard and high to Trueman standing in the gully. Trueman threw up a hand and deflected it high in the air. It dropped between him and his neighbour, Bailey. I have no desire to analyse a complicated situation, but between the two the ball fell to the ground, Trueman finishing the effort on the grass.

Trueman was replaced by Wardle. Statham, bowling "tight", continued awhile; his first seven overs had cost only six runs, but presently spin bowling, from Wardle and Titmus, took charge at both ends. Twice in three balls did McLean drive Titmus to the boundary; the second of these strokes was just too high for May at mid-off to reach.

Titmus became rather expensive. Five fours, three to McLean and two to Keith, were hit from him in three overs. McLean, showing no sign of nerves at 99, tapped the single right away to clinch his century. He had scored it in 160 minutes, hitting a six and fourteen fours. This was the first century in the present series, and the second in McLean's Test career. The other was hit against New Zealand.

The 200 was passed and still the partnership flourished despite sundry changes of bowlers. Wardle was hit for two successive fours by McLean, and May turned over to the delayed new ball. Another chance went west when Keith was missed by Titmus low down in the gully off the long-suffering Statham.

McLean's long innings was ended just before lunch by Statham. He played at the ball too late, and it took the top of his middle stump. Two hundred and forty-seven for six—a lead now of 114. In his three and a half hours' batting for 142 runs McLean had hit a six and 21 fours.

During lunch time there was unconscious humour in a loud-speaker appeal to spectators to keep behind the boundary rope "in order to give the fieldsmen every chance of making a catch".

Keith and Mansell scored 12 together before a slip catch was held by Graveney at Mansell's expense. The fieldsman juggled with the ball, but held on, and Wardle had the wicket.

Keith and Tayfield took the South African total to more than twice our own 133. Keith reached his 50 after batting three hours and hitting seven widely separated boundaries. Tayfield, after sundry narrow escapes in just failing to touch balls from Statham, fell not to that bowler but to Titmus, whose first Test wicket this was. Tayfield tried a big hit to leg and was bowled. He and Keith had added 43.

The end of the innings was now at hand. Keith and Heine both fell to Wardle in one over. The catch which dismissed Keith was a specially brilliant one, for the catcher, Titmus, took the ball very low down on the run.

Statham deserved a far better harvest of wickets than a mere two, which cost his side no more than 49 runs in 27 overs. By comparison the bowling of Trueman, taker also of two wickets, lacked control. Wardle came along with four wickets in the middle and end of the innings.

England in their second innings again made a disheartening beginning. Kenyon and Graveney, facing a deficit of 171, were parted with the total only nine. Goddard, who had just suc-ceeded Adcock, had Kenyon l.b.w. when he kneed away a ball.

The rest of the day's story was much happier for England.

Graveney and May, without being parted, took the total to 108 for one wicket. Goddard had a long spell of his tantalising

left-hand bowling, directed chiefly on the leg side. At the other
end Heine and Adcock shared the bowling until Tayfield had a
turn for the first time late in the day.

Each of our batsmen reached his 50 and at the close, 108
for one, our deficit had been pared down to 63.

THIRD DAY

*England's second innings was expanded to 353 all out,
leaving South Africa 183 to make to win the match. At
close of play they had scored 17 for two wickets.*

This was a Saturday, and Londoners made of it quite an
"Australia" day. Nearly 30,000 people packed the ground,
and the gates were shut. Long before play began attendants
were moving round the ground trying to keep the chalked
boundary lines clear. Lord's, by the way, ought to have, in
those parts of the ground where the public are allowed on the
grass, some less flimsy barrier than one sagging rope which is
really no barrier at all. I know that a fixed fence cannot be
erected over the grass, but it ought not to be beyond human
ingenuity to solve the trouble.

Adcock had strained a leg muscle the previous day, but he
opened the bowling with Heine. Off him Graveney scored the
single which completed the hundred stand after a partnership
of two hours and twenty minutes. To begin with the scoring was
very slow, and May did not seem happy against Adcock, who
was bowling flat out without apparent discomfort. Only 12
runs were scored in the first half hour, but then there came an
over from Heine, yielding a boundary to Graveney and another
to May, with an intervening single. After 40 minutes Adcock
was succeeded by the industrious left-hander Goddard, who is
able to bowl most of the day at small cost.

When May hit Heine for two more boundaries in the same
over we came within 30 of wiping off arrears. Then Graveney,
who in three-quarters of an hour had added only seven to his
overnight 53, was out. He tried to speed up a ball from
Goddard on his leg side and half hit it to Heine, fielding close

behind the bat. Graveney had batted for 200 minutes and had hit five fours. He and May had put on 132.

Compton joined May and the scoring rate quickened. May cover-drove Heine for four again, and Compton hooked Goddard for four and cut him for three. When Tayfield had his first bowl of the day Compton off-drove his first ball for another boundary. So the Englishmen did wipe out the arrears of 171, and every run after that was on the credit side.

Four byes off Tayfield and a cover-drive by May over McGlew's head helped things along nicely. May was not having everything his own way against Tayfield. Once he was beaten and nearly bowled, but he then hit another cover-drive, this one at ground level, to the feet of the boundary sitters.

The 200 total arrived in just the same lucky way as the 171— four more byes off Tayfield past Compton. Then May completed his fourth Test Match century, scored out of 206 made whilst he was at the wicket for four hours and ten minutes. He reached his distinction spectacularly by driving Tayfield straight to the only sight-screen Lord's employs. He had hit 16 fours. This was his 44th century in first-class cricket, and one of his best. His first real escape came when slow bowler Mansell was given a caught and bowled chance low down which he did not accept.

The new ball was taken and some of the shine left it when May hit Adcock for two more boundaries. Visions of an indefinite English lead arose, but then May's innings ended in misfortune. He trod on his wicket. As he played back to a ball from Heine his left heel just touched the leg-stump and the bail fell off. This was a luckless end to an innings of 112, for which May had been batting four and a half hours.

Next in was Barrington. Soon after he arrived a late cut by Compton off Adcock, all grace and delicacy, rounded off his half century in an hour and a half of batting. One never tires of watching Compton. I think the stroke which delights me most is that short-armed hook of his, taken close to the body with next to no back-swing of the bat. He produced a sample again at Heine's expense, and the rocket-like path taken by the ball to the boundary made one marvel at the strength of the Comptonian biceps.

Barrington was content to play second fiddle to the great man, but stayed while 40 runs were made and produced the stroke which took our lead into three figures. He was out fourth at 277 in hooking Tayfield. McLean caught him at square leg.

So to Bailey as Compton's next partner. When he had made six there was a consultation between the umpires about him. The point at issue was the validity of a catch at second slip. Gray invited an opinion from Chester at the other end. Chester could not give Bailey out and he remained at the wicket. A minute later, however, Mansell in the slips caught Compton off Goddard.

Compton, out for 69, had batted two and a half hours with 11 fours. I will not say that this innings was as brilliant as those he was destined to play later in the Manchester Test, but it was the innings the occasion demanded. Two hundred and eighty-five for five.

Evans stayed with Bailey while 17 were added, and then hit a return catch to Tayfield. Wardle managed only a common or garden boundary for four instead of his usual six off Tayfield. Next he tried to do better and Heine near the sight-screen held the ball while tumbling over with the momentum of his run. Three hundred and six for seven.

Titmus gave Bailey useful help before Waite caught him acrobatically behind the wicket. Bailey himself fell to Tayfield and Statham and Trueman made minor contributions. The innings closed for 353.

The South Africans had about 35 minutes' batting and McGlew was l.b.w. for a duck to Statham's first delivery. Seventeen runs were added and then Statham had the other opener, Goddard, caught by Evans behind the wicket. In four overs that evening Statham took two wickets for eight runs. At the end of the day the South Africans with eight wickets in hand needed 166 for victory. The task, as it happened, was beyond them.

It might not have been beyond them if the last ball of that Saturday's play, bowled by Trueman, had not hit Cheetham seriously on the left elbow. That misfortune may well have been the turning point of the match, for Cheetham took no further part in it.

FOURTH DAY

*South Africa were all out for 111 runs, and England
won by 71 at 5 p.m., with the next day to spare.*

Statham was again the bowler to clinch the match for
England. His Saturday analysis of two wickets for eight runs
was expanded on this Monday to seven wickets for 39—a piece
of fast bowling as good as anything I have seen for years.
Statham is so essentially accurate in his bowling, and so essentially fair. He is always attacking the wicket rather than the
batsman.

For nearly an hour the over-night batsman, Tayfield, held
up his end in company with the newcomer Endean, who had
taken the place of his injured captain. These two added 23 to the
overnight 17 for two, Tayfield's share a modest three. At last
the admirable Statham, whose first five overs of the day had
been maidens, had Tayfield groping, not by any means for the
first time. Now he made an offering to Evans behind the wicket
and the total became 40 for three. All through that hour of
resistance Tayfield was stubbing the turf with his right big
toe in his usual staccato manner. I wondered whether he knew
he was doing it, or whether the habit has by now become so
ingrained as to be second nature.

Both our fast bowlers, Statham and Trueman, had been
making the ball lift. Indeed once Trueman, pitching it at
Tayfield's feet, produced quite a weird effect. It must have
"hit something" for it cleared Evans's head as well as the
batsman's and streaked off to the boundary.

During this partnership Endean gave what seemed to be a
good low chance to Titmus in the gully and the fieldsman held
on. Gray consulted Chester, as he had two days previously over
Bailey, and again the batsman remained in. McLean, century
maker of the first innings, joined Endean and had just broken
his duck when an astonishing interruption occurred. Now, at
high noon, an umbrella of black cloud gathered and remained
stationary over Lord's, extending the luncheon break to two
hours. The umpires had no alternative but to stop play.

Hardly ever can Lord's have had such an interruption in the

middle of June. Everyone expected a deluge at any moment, and the whole paraphernalia of appliances for protecting everything except the playing surface was kept at the ready. The rain, however, was never enough to do any serious damage, or even to drive the big crowd to shelter.

When at last the umpires, on whose initiative the game had been suspended, decided it should be resumed, the light was still poor, but improved. McLean, cutting Trueman for four, brought the total to 50, but four runs later Statham took the wicket which the Englishmen most wanted. McLean was thoroughly beaten and bowled. Fifty-four for four, and Statham now four wickets for 19.

Endean over and over again looked like giving a catch off Statham, either to Evans or to the slips. Statham was bowling so close to the wicket that the batsman dared not risk leaving the ball alone. He got Endean at last with a catch tipped to Evans. Sixty-three for five; Statham five for 21.

Keith, now partnering Waite, groped at Statham almost as badly as if that black cloud had persisted. If everyone who tried to make contact that day had succeeded Statham's analysis would have been even better than it was.

Waite and Keith added 12 anxious runs before Statham gained his next wicket. He had Waite l.b.w. Seventy-five for six, Statham six for 30. But he could not take "all ten", for the batting side were one short. Cheetham could only sit in the pavilion, arm in sling, and wistfully watch.

Statham in ordinary circumstances would have been given a rest, for he was in danger of "bowling himself into the ground", but when a man is taking wickets as quickly as this his captain just hates to take him off. Keith at 78 was the next player to go, the result of a tumbling catch in the slips by Graveney.

Mansell and Heine took more conquering. Indeed, they increased the score from 78 to 111, with Heine for once content to defend. It is all against his instincts, however, to do this indefinitely and at last he hit out at Wardle and was splendidly caught by Kenyon right on the edge of the boundary. This wicket by Wardle was the first taken by any bowler other than Statham.

With Adcock the last man in Mansell realised that the game was up and tried a big hit on his own account. Kenyon, whose part in the match had been limited to three runs and some good work in the outfield, now became prominent again with a second high catch, more difficult than the first. He held on, however, and a splendid game was over. What would have been the result if Cheetham's injury had not disorganised the South African innings? Here your guess is as good as mine.

The game was conspicuous not only for its fluctuating fortunes, but for its many adventures and the good-tempered spirit in which it was played.

England were now two victories to love up in the rubber of five.

Full scores are as follows:

ENGLAND

First Innings

D. Kenyon b Adcock	1
T. W. Graveney c Waite b Heine	15
P. B. H. May c Tayfield b Heine	0
D. C. S. Compton c Keith b Heine	20
K. Barrington b Heine	34
T. E. Bailey lbw b Goddard	13
T. G. Evans c Waite b Heine	20
F. Titmus lbw b Goddard	4
J. H. Wardle c Tayfield b Goddard	20
J. B. Statham c McLean b Goddard	0
F. Trueman not out	2
Extras	4
Total	133

Fall of Wickets

1—7; 2—8; 3—30; 4—45; 5—62; 6—98; 7—111; 8—111; 9—111.

Compton is dropped
by Keith, off Heine,
during the first day
at Old Trafford

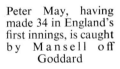

Peter May, having
made 34 in England's
first innings, is caught
by Mansell off
Goddard

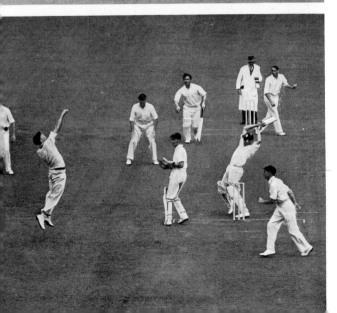

Bailey the stonewaller
at last "has a go",
and cracks the ball
hard past the leaping
fieldsman

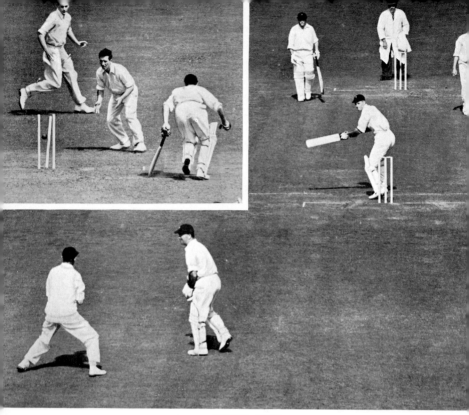

THIRD TEST

(*Top left*): Goddard just gets home, as a smart throw-in by Lock on the boundary shatters the wicket.　(*Top right*): This time Goddard is not so lucky, and is caught by Graveney off Tyson after making 62.　(*Bottom left*): Evans, England's wicketkeeper, who had broken a finger, gives a hint or two to his temporary successor, Tom Graveney, before the start of the fourth day's play.　(*Bottom right*): Kenyon makes a fine catch to dismiss Waite off Bedser for 113

BOWLING

	O.	M.	R.	W.
Heine	25	7	60	5
Adcock	8	3	10	1
Goddard	21·2	8	59	4

SOUTH AFRICA

FIRST INNINGS

D. J. McGlew c Evans b Statham	0
T. L. Goddard c Evans b Trueman	0
J. E. Cheetham lbw b Bailey	13
W. R. Endean lbw b Wardle	48
R. A. McLean b Statham	142
J. H. B. Waite c Evans b Trueman	8
H. J. Keith c Titmus b Wardle	57
P. N. F. Mansell c Graveney b Wardle	2
H. J. Tayfield b Titmus	21
P. Heine, st Evans b Wardle	2
N. A. T. Adcock not out	0
Extras	11
Total	304

FALL OF WICKETS

1—0; 2—7; 3—51; 4—101; 5—138; 6—247; 7—259; 8—302; 9—304.

BOWLING

	O.	M.	R.	W.
Statham	27	9	49	2
Trueman	16	2	73	2
Bailey	16	2	56	1
Wardle	29	10	65	4
Titmus	14	3	50	1

E

ENGLAND

Second Innings

D. Kenyon lbw b Goddard	.. .. ..	2
T. W. Graveney c Heine b Goddard	.. ..	60
P. B. H. May, hw b Heine	.. .. ..	112
D. C. S. Compton c Mansell b Goddard	.. ..	69
K. Barrington c McLean b Tayfield	.. ..	18
T. E. Bailey c Adcock b Tayfield	.. .. ..	22
T. G. Evans c and b Tayfield	.. .. ..	14
J. H. Wardle c Heine b Tayfield	.. .. ..	4
F. Titmus c Waite b Adcock	.. .. ..	16
J. B. Statham b Tayfield	.. .. ..	11
F. Trueman not out	.. ..	19
Extras	.. .. ..	19
Total	.. .. ..	353

Fall of Wickets

1—9; 2—141; 3—237; 4—277; 5—285; 6—302; 7—306; 8—336; 9—336.

Bowling

		O.	M.	R.	W.
Heine	.. ..	29	5	87	1
Adcock	.. ..	25	5	64	1
Goddard	.. ..	55	23	96	3
Tayfield	.. ..	38·5	12	80	5
Mansell	.. ..	2	0	7	0

SOUTH AFRICA

SECOND INNINGS

D. J. McGlew lbw b Statham	..	..	..		0
T. L. Goddard c Evans b Statham		..	..		10
J. E. Cheetham retired hurt	..	..	..		3
H. J. Tayfield c Evans b Statham	..	..	..		3
W. R. Endean c Evans b Statham	..		..		28
R. A. McLean b Statham	..	..	..		8
H. J. Keith c Graveney b Statham		..	..		5
J. H. B. Waite lbw b Statham	..		..		9
P. N. F. Mansell c Kenyon b Wardle		..	..		16
P. Heine c Kenyon b Wardle	..		..		14
N. A. T. Adcock not out	..	..	..		0
Extras	..	..	..	..	15
Total	..	..	..	..	111

FALL OF WICKETS

1—0; 2—17; 3—40; 4—54; 5—63; 6—75; 7—78; 8—111;
9—111.

BOWLING

	O.	M.	R.	W.
Statham	..	29	12	39	7
Trueman	..	19	2	39	0
Wardle	..	9·4	4	18	2

England won by 71 runs.

CHAPTER VII

YORKSHIRE MASTERED

FROM Lord's the South Africans moved first to Northampton and then to Sheffield. In each case they showed improving form. Against Northants they had the better of a draw; and, much more to their credit, they beat Yorkshire.

A feature of the game in the Midlands was a century by C. A. R. Duckworth, the reserve wicketkeeper. Men who fill this position always have my sympathy. Usually they are given just about enough work to keep them in practice, and no more than that. Everyone knows that unless the keeper-in-chief is ill or injured Test Match play is not for them. Before this Northampton game Duckworth, who at 22 was the youngest member of the party, had played in four matches and had missed eight. His highest score had been 15; yet in this game, right in mid-season, he blossomed out into innings of 158 and 30 not out. As a result he was in the "short list" as a batsman for the Third Test, but was not chosen.

Against Northants this big effort by Duckworth and substantial ones by Goddard and Mansell took the South African total to 409. Northants managed to save the follow-on with 271, in which the chief item was 70 by Subba Row, previously well-known in the Surrey side. South Africans went out for victory with a second innings declaration at 80 for one, but again Subba Row stood in their way. The match ended when Northants scored 133 for four.

Yorkshire at one time had quite a chance of winning, for in reply to the South Africans 209 Lowson and Watson, each with a half century, gave the County a fine start. But Tayfield and Heine were too good for the rest of the side and the absence of Hutton was sorely felt. In the South African second innings nearly everyone made runs, and they totalled 360.

Yorkshire lost the match by 193 runs and would have been much worse defeated if Johnnie Wardle had not sailed in with a characteristic effort at number eight in the batting list. He hit his first 50 in 18 minutes and scored 74 out of 85 in half an hour before Tayfield bowled him.

This victory over Yorkshire, then running Surrey closely for the championship, was probably the turning point in the tour. Before it happened the South Africans, well as they had performed against most of the other counties, were by no means sure how they would fare against those near the top. The record of previous sides against Yorkshire was not satisfactory. Fourteen matches had been played by South African touring parties against the Northerners. Two had been won, one lost, and the other eleven drawn. Their victory now enabled them to turn towards the third Test Match with confidence.

For this Third Test played at Old Trafford, Manchester, both teams had changes, some of them voluntary, some made necessary by injury. The English side varied in four instances from the victorious one of Lord's. Barrington gave way to Cowdrey, who in the brief period since his release from the R.A.F. had shown that there was nothing the matter with his cricket, whatever the condition of his feet. Lock came into the side for the first time in place of Wardle.

During these early Tests Statham and Tyson were doing a sort of Cox and Box Act. Now it was Statham's turn to be injured and Tyson's to play. Trueman, too, was injured—he had strained himself while bowling for his County at Bournemouth—and back into the English side was welcomed Alec Bedser. The same Bedser as had played for his country in 47 Tests; indeed, until he was dropped after the first match of the recent series in Australia his choice for every English side against every country had been automatic. Only when he was not present, as during the tour in the West Indies, was he left out. He holds the Test record of 232 wickets, and he has bowled more balls for England than anyone else. For sentimental, as well as practical, reasons it was good to see him at Headingley.

Note how quickly the personnel of these English teams changes. Even now with the series only three matches old, the number of players performing in them all was limited to six—Bailey, May, Compton, Evans, Graveney and Kenyon. When,

a little later, the side for the Fourth Test was chosen Evans and
Kenyon vanished from the scene, Evans because he was
injured and Kenyon because he was dropped.

In addition to these six, seven others had played in one or
more of the earlier Tests—Appleyard, Barrington, Statham,
Tyson, Titmus, Wardle and Trueman. So, including Cowdrey,
no fewer than fourteen players had been called into service for
England—in a side, mark you, which up to then was victorious.
The survivors of the "victory" Test which won the Ashes for us
at Adelaide were only six—May, Cowdrey, Compton, Bailey,
Evans, Tyson.

Here is the eleven which took the field at Manchester:
Kenyon, Graveney, May, Compton, Cowdrey, Bailey, Titmus,
Evans, Lock, Tyson, Bedser.

The South African side had only one change, Winslow in
place of the injured Cheetham, and McGlew took over the
captaincy. Their side was thus: McGlew, Goddard, Keith,
Mansell, Endean, McLean, Waite, Winslow, Tayfield, Heine,
Adcock. Mansell's position must have been in some doubt,
for he had made very poor contributions with the bat and
had bowled only two overs in the previous Test Match. Pre-
sumably he was retained because of his excellence as a slip
fieldsman.

By now the only men picked for all Test Matches were
McGlew, Goddard, Endean, McLean, Waite, Tayfield and
Adcock. Seven others, Cheetham, Fuller, Heine, Keith,
Mansell, Smith and Winslow had played in one or more
matches.

A factor which had immensely improved the South
Africans as a side was the belated advent of real summer
weather. They seemed a different crowd of fellows directly the
sun shone on their backs, and they were able to take the field
without sweaters. The change from the depressing chill of
June and early July made an astounding difference in their
performances.

Here Manchester did them proud. Never have I known
the great Northern capital so pleasantly warm, so unfailingly
dry, since the famous match against the Australians in 1934.
I seem to remember—though of course I may be wrong—that

on that occasion Mancunians were rolling up at Old Trafford in shorts, pith helmets and safari jackets. I remember Tom Webster's amusing cartoon about tropical Manchester. We have been paying heavily there for that experience ever since until now.

CHAPTER VIII

THE THIRD TEST MATCH

*Played at Old Trafford, Manchester, on 7th, 8th, 9th, 11th
and 12th July, and won by South Africa by three wickets at
6.25 on the fifth day.*

FIRST DAY

*May won the toss for England for the third time
running, decided to bat and England scored 264 for seven
in the first six hours of the match. It was a dull day's
play apart from the brilliance of Denis Compton, who
at the close of the day had made 155 not out, far more than
all the other batsmen added together.*

THE match began in curious weather for Manchester—
fine, warm, humid, calm, overcast, with a strange haze over
the ground which blurred the stumps as seen from the ringside.
This haze had not dispersed when McGlew led his men out,
but it did not persist very long.

Two singles to Kenyon were the sum total of our scoring in
the first quarter of an hour, and then Graveney fell for a duck.
He turned the ball smartly from Adcock's fast bowling to Tayfield, one of the leg slips standing fairly close in. May, who is
used to coming in in this situation, saw a ball pass behind his
legs for four byes, then got off the mark with a single. Facing
the next over from the tremendous Heine he drove him for
three past a non-existent long-on.

Then came the best stroke so far from anyone, a square
cut to the boundary by May, all wrist and timing. After 35
minutes, with the score 22 Kenyon rounded off the failure of the
opening pair by being caught at the wicket when flashing at
Heine.

So to a partnership between May and Compton which

mended matters considerably. Compton's first run was a streak
of luck for him. He turned the ball waist high only just wide of
Heine's far-flung left hand—at the end of a very long arm—
for one run. It was not an actual chance, but was not very far
from it. Compton was not overawed by his escape or by the
crisis. He received a ball from Heine which capered over his
left shoulder. Instead of letting it go, as many a batsman would
so early in his innings, he did a sort of two-handed tennis smash
for one run.

May continued to bat with the utmost promise, and runs
came along at rather better than one a minute. The fast
bowlers remained in action for nearly an hour, and then were
replaced by Tayfield, slow off-breaks, and Goddard, left-hand
medium-pace.

The cricket became quiet, though now and then there was
a productive stroke such as a boundary by May past slip and a
four and a three to Compton. Twenty minutes before lunch this
partnership, which had advanced the score from 22 to 70, was
ended. May tried another of those glorious off-drives of his
at Goddard's expense, but only half-hit the ball, which he
edged into the hands of Mansell in the gully. May had scored
34, including five fours, and Compton was then 23. The stand
had lasted an hour.

Cowdrey did not endure long in his first innings of this
series. After taking a single from Goddard he played forward in
defence to Tayfield. The ball probably went "straight on"
instead of turning, and Mansell was given another catch off the
edge of the bat. Seventy-five for four.

Now at this early stage in the match Bailey was in action
with Compton. It was a very un-Bailey-like beginning to his
innings, for he twice slashed Tayfield to the boundary. The
half-clad boundary boys, kept in order by coatless policemen
in the heat, cheered themselves hoarse. We were at least a little
better off than at Lord's, where the first five English wickets
fell for 62.

After lunch Compton and Bailey reached the hundred
total, which had taken the side two and a half hours to compile.
Compton did most of the scoring, while Bailey also served by
standing and waiting. The next milestone along this difficult

road was Compton's 50, which he reached with fours hooked off Heine and Tayfield Another stroke, similar in character, from the same batsman after a while rounded off the half-century partnership, towards which Bailey, in an hour and five minutes, had made 15.

Manchester serves its on-the-field refreshments in style. There was a time, I remember, when a butler attired in tails, boiled shirt and dignity used to carry out the drinks. In the more recent match the orange and water was borne by the South African twelfth man, a male attendant in black trousers and white coat, and two white-capped maids with fluttering apron strings. My friend the cartoonist, Roy Ullyett of the *Daily Express*, just could not miss an opportunity like this. One of the girls was depicted asking "Ethel", the other one, whether they received England caps for this performance.

When he made 58 Compton gave a hard chance to Keith in the gully off Heine. The scoring hereabouts grew very slow, for neither Tayfield nor Goddard allowed any liberties. They were relieved by Mansell, who bowls leg-spinners, and Keith, slow left-hand. Still runs did not arrive quickly.

Compton, hitting Keith for a boundary, reached his hundred. Bailey, after three hours at the wicket, hooked his last two boundaries and then gave a catch at the wicket to Waite, bowling with the new ball. Two hundred and nineteen for five —a stand of 144.

With Titmus in Compton was again missed, this time off Heine, whom he proceeded to hit for three fours. Both Titmus and Evans were out to Heine runless, and seven wickets were down for 242 runs. We should indeed have been in a terrible way had it not been for the Compton-Bailey stand.

Lock played out time with Compton, who at the close of play had been batting for four and a quarter hours. He had come to the wicket with the total only 22, which meant that his 155 had been scored out of 242 runs collected while he was at the wicket. A tremendous performance on his part. The pity of it was he was not given better support.

SECOND DAY

*England were all out for 284 to which South Africa
replied with 199 for four wickets.*

This undoubtedly was South Africa's day. Compton's
innings ended with the addition of only three more runs.
Then after our dismissal for a modest total the South African
openers, McGlew and Goddard, had an opening partnership
of 147.

The day was sunny but the heat was tempered by a breeze.
In Australia one becomes used to shirt-sleeved men and lightly
clad women around the ring at cricket-grounds. To see this
at Manchester, and again a fortnight later at Leeds, restored
one's faith, of late sadly shattered, in the English summer.
Manchester's reputation was redeemed.

Lock had gone in overnight to help Compton complete
the day without further casualties. He is no sort of dolt with the
bat, this big Surrey slow bowler. He out-lived Compton and
the two tail-enders, Tyson and Bedser, for a well-played 19 not
out.

Compton's scoring strokes that day were only two. The first
of them gave him two runs off Goddard through the clustering
leg-side fieldsmen. Presently he took another single, but after a
quarter of an hour he raised his bat defensively to a ball which
I believe would have cleared the top of his off-stump. The ball,
bowled by Adcock, may have swung away from him a trifle,
and he gave Waite, the wicketkeeper, a catch.

The scoreboard now read 271 for eight, last man 158.
Subtract from 271 the 22 scored before Compton came in and
you realize how he had shouldered our innings. He had batted
just over five and a half hours and had hit 22 fours. During his
innings he had been missed four times, but he deserved his
luck.

Directly Tyson joined Lock the Surrey bowler was missed in
the slips. The South African slip fielding in this innings was
hardly better than was ours at Lord's. Tyson scored only two
towards a little partnership of nine with Lock, and then he was
bowled by Goddard.

Alec Bedser had a reception which sounded to me more enthusiastic than that given to Compton himself. Crowds in the North, as well as the South, have taken to the big Surrey bowler, so tireless and so great a trier whether things are going well or badly. He did not play a long innings, but after scoring a single was l.b.w. to Goddard.

The innings was over for 284 after forty minutes' cricket that day.

When the South African innings began, with just over an hour's batting before lunch, Bedser was given the new ball, which McGlew hit for four off the very first delivery. Tyson's first ball from the other end also produced four runs. Apparently it hit something or other, for it sailed high over the head of Evans to the boundary at express speed for four byes. The pace at which this ball was bowled was prodigious, to judge from the way it bounded in the air after striking one of the parked wicket-covers behind the boundary line.

All the first ten runs from the bat were scored by McGlew. Goddard followed with a single, and South Africa at least had improved on the performance of England the day before. The openers stood up very well to the expresses of Tyson and the swingers of Bedser. Once Goddard withdrew himself and his bat from a ball from Tyson which passed him chest high. An appeal from half a dozen voices for a catch behind the wicket was answered unfavourably by umpire Dai Davies.

Tyson bowled for five overs and forty minutes for 14 runs and then Bailey took over from him with the total 40. McGlew brought up a brisk 50 total by driving Bedser for two boundaries in one over. Bedser's opening spell of eight overs cost 31 runs, and Lock bowled a solitary over in his stead just before lunch, taken at 60 for no wicket, McGlew 31, Goddard 24.

After lunch there was a tranquil period, shattered when a yell of appeal went up against Goddard for a supposed chance to Evans. The umpire had no need to answer it because the wicketkeeper dropped the ball. Graveney, standing at first slip, picked it up and quite justifiably gave away two overthrows in trying to run out Goddard at the opposite end.

Lock bowled his first five overs for 1 run, and appealed for l.b.w. against McGlew, with the same result as previous appeals. Lock after this became a trifle less inexpensive and McGlew completed his third 50 of the series. It had taken him just over two hours. Not long afterwards the 100 partnership arrived. Titmus had been bowling by now, in addition to Tyson, Bedser, Bailey and Lock. I wondered why Compton was not given a trial—or Graveney. These occasional bowlers can be costly, but they surely are worth trying for two or three overs when the regular men have bowled in vain. The batsman is apt to grow careless, take a chance and get himself out.

A first-class opportunity of ending this stubborn stand occurred before tea when McGlew tried to drive a ball from Titmus over the head of mid-on. He lifted a skier to Bedser, who, although not mobile these days, is a pretty safe fieldsman to anything coming straight to him as this one did. He seemed to be bringing off the catch all right, but the ball passed through his hands to earth. This was when McGlew had scored 68 and the total was 122.

After tea the stand was ended at last when it had yielded 147 runs. Goddard was caught in the slips by Graveney off Tyson. He had made 62.

In came Keith and almost immediately McGlew was seen walking to the pavilion. He had taken two or three knocks on the right hand and went off to a doctor for an X-ray. His score at the time was 77 and he did not bat again that day. His retirement seemed to disorganize the innings. Keith and Mansell became slow and the English bowling, after flagging during the long first partnership, took the initiative again. Mansell was l.b.w. to Lock at 171, after three-quarters of an hour, and Endean who never was happy was out to the Evans-Lock combination. At 182 McLean was bowled by Tyson. So it happened that while the first wicket did not fall until the total was 147 four batsmen were out only 35 runs later.

The capture of McLean after only a quarter of an hour's batting was particularly pleasing to the Englishmen. Keith and Waite were still in at the end of the day.

THIRD DAY

*South Africa's total was increased from 199 for four to
482 for seven.*

A weary day this was for the England bowlers, who all day
long could take only three wickets while 283 runs were added
to the hostile total. It was by no means all the fault of the
bowlers, for our fieldsmen let them down badly. Never since
the First Test at Brisbane last November had I seen the
England attack take such a drubbing.

The weather was still sunny, but no longer as hot as before,
for a brisk breeze felt quite chilly in the shade. Tyson, bowling
with it in his favour, was no nice adversary for any batsman
to face. His first ball hit the right thigh of the left-hander
Keith, not out 22 overnight, and there followed two singles
from the rest of the over.

Bedser's luck in Test cricket is right out. Off his very first
ball of the day Waite gave Graveney a chance at first slip,
but the ball went down. The next ball was steered rather flukily
by Waite for four wide of Lock at fine leg.

Tyson's pace is so great that the deflective strokes on both
sides of the wicket carry tremendous speed. Bailey, trying to
stop a leg glide by Waite, went to earth in an attempt to save
the four, but the ball sped through his hands and dribbled into
touch. In a quarter of an hour the batsmen, aided by a cover-
drive for four by Keith off Bedser, raised the overnight total
by 17. Our score of 284 was obviously going to be left far behind.

Tyson's first spell, lasting three-quarters of an hour, failed
in its purpose and Bailey replaced him. Bedser went on longer
before being succeeded by Lock.

After an hour and a quarter's play a wicket fell at last.
Bailey was bowling well and Keith, in trying to square-drive
him, gave a chance in the slips. Graveney got into position for
the catch by taking a step or two to his left and this time secured
the ball at chest height.

It was a long long time indeed before another wicket came
our way. Waite was now 42, and Winslow joined him in a
stand raising the score from 245 to 416.

Soon after Winslow arrived Waite completed his 50. Winslow—the man who hit Jack Ikin of Lancashire for 30 in an over—was deprived of his first four by a smart piece of fielding by the stumps at the other end. Deciding to avoid them next time Winslow lifted the ball from Bailey for the first six of the match, an on-drive which gave the throng among whom the ball fell the greatest delight.

Tyson was bowling again before lunch and a leg-glide off him by Waite brought South Africa within five of the lead. Directly after lunch Winslow secured it by hooking the ball over the head of mid-wicket for four, at Lock's expense. For good measure he off-drove the next for the same value.

The Manchester crowd was a splendidly sporting one, giving every good stroke by the South Africans its full applause. The cheering reached tornado force—or should I say typhoon force?—when Tyson was deflected by Winslow for a three down the leg side which brought the total to 300. Tyson's afternoon opening spell was no more successful than his morning one, and Titmus was brought on in his place. When Waite had made 61 a regular male voice choir was upraised in appeal against him for a catch behind the wicket. Umpire Frank Lee turned it down.

Hereabouts Titmus had much the same bad luck as had Bedser earlier in the innings. Winslow gave Tyson a chance of a catch at deep mid-on. It was not easy, for the fieldsman had to run in an awkward cross-direction under the ball. The chance went down and Winslow celebrated the fact by hitting the young bowler for a two, a six and two fours. It was a heartbreaking experience for a player so new to Test cricket.

Winslow, although not scoring at hurricane speed right through his innings, was yet on occasions hitting the ball tremendously hard. He reached his 100 just before tea in the grand manner. The stroke which took him from 96 to 102 was one of the longest six-hits I have seen for many a year. It carried the ball over the sight-screen on to an awning behind it, and thence into the car-park. Winslow had left Waite far behind in the quest of a century. Indeed Winslow was out to the new ball bowled by Bedser, before Waite reached it. Four hundred and sixteen for six.

Waite had gone to the wicket nearly half an hour before the close of play on the previous day and now his patient innings was not over until nearly six o'clock. The crowd liked best, as all crowds do, the sixes of Winslow, hit with that free swinging bat of his, yet Waite's innings was of equal value to his side. It was ended by a fine diving catch by Kenyon at mid-on, and Bedser had secured the wicket of both century-makers.

Tayfield and McGlew, who had resumed his innings from his 77 not out, with the knowledge that no bones in his hand were broken, prevented any further fall of wickets that day.

FOURTH DAY

South Africa declared their innings closed at 521 for eight, a lead of 237. England in the second innings scored 250 for four wickets.

The day's cricket was distinguished by a stand of 124 runs by Peter May and Denis Compton which made us feel that defeat for England was not quite a foregone conclusion. But first the close of the South African innings. It was completed on a day in which Manchester could compare itself with Melbourne in summertime discomfort.

England took the field that Monday under a tremendous disadvantage, for Evans was unable to keep wicket. For much of the Saturday he had been doing so in acute pain. A ball from Tyson had broken the little finger of his left hand, and it was in plaster. Who was to deputise? No one in the side had any worth-while experience, but Tom Graveney volunteered and was accepted. He told me that his last appearance behind the stumps was at a one-day charity match down in Gloucestershire some years before. His experience of wicket-keeping indeed, as he admitted himself, was negligible.

Graveney was given a brief "trial trip" at the nets by some of the Englishmen, aided by two or three of the South Africans. But you cannot make a Godfrey Evans in a quarter of an hour. It would be no bad plan if some member of the Test side were earmarked as emergency wicketkeeper; his County could be

A trio of South African century makers at Old Trafford, photographed after the visitors had declared. They are (*left to right*): Waite, McGlew, and Winslow

THIRD TEST

Compton looks apprehensive as he is about to be caught by Mansell off Heine for 71 in England's second innings

While McLean and McGlew are both at the same end May runs out McLean, nevertheless, South Africa won the third Test with five minutes to spare

South African batsman Endean (*right*) collides with Wardle in his haste to reach the crease

McIntyre, the England wicketkeeper (*below*), catches out McGlew of South Africa after the latter had snicked at a ball from Loader

May hits a ball which sends two opponents sprawling in an effort to stop it

encouraged to give him practice now and then at unimportant moments in their matches. I remember once that Frank Woolley, who did pretty well everything in cricket with distinction except keep wicket, had to take on the job in a Test against Australia. It really was not fair on him.

The crowd gave Graveney a cheer for his first stop behind the stumps to Tyson's bowling. Bailey was fielding at deep leg so very fine that he was almost a long stop, and Lock, fielding near the wicket, was ever ready to run in quickly and take returns from the field.

McGlew, 89 not out overnight, hooked Bailey, bowling opposite to Tyson, for a boundary which took him into his nineties. He had a slice of luck in the form of five runs resulting from an overthrow. The ball was aimed at the stumps with every justification by Parkhouse, the twelfth man; McGlew, it seemed from the ring, would have been out if the ball had hit the target.

A minute later a single to McGlew off Bailey gave the batsman the third century of this mammoth South African innings, and the first scored by McGlew himself in this series. Thus far he had batted four hours and twenty minutes on three different days and had hit nineteen fours. Immediately afterwards Tayfield was bowled by Tyson after long resistance. Four hundred and ninety-eight for eight, and Heine came in to join McGlew.

The five hundredth run came up amid applause from the crowd as hearty as though the feat had been England's. Heine, who loves to "have a go" and possesses the necessary physique, hit Lock for three fours and a single in one over, though one of the boundaries had in it more good luck than good management. Throughout this innings Lock had bowled well with atrocious ill-fortune.

A single added by McGlew in the same over was the last run, for the acting captain closed the innings at 521 for eight with his own score 104 not out, and that of Heine 22 not out. The innings had lasted about eleven and a half hours. It had occupied only forty minutes of the fourth day.

Once again England's innings opened disappointingly. After only quarter of an hour Graveney was bowled by Adcock when

F

late with his stroke. Graveney had scored only 1 and the total was 2. Kenyon survived his partner for only five minutes without addition to the score. Then he raised his bat defensively to a sharp riser from Heine. He glanced the ball into the wicketkeeper's gloves. So already, after only twenty minutes, May and Compton were brought together. They faced the bowling with no apparent difficulty and made boundary strokes off both Adcock and Heine. In their first half hour together they put on 37 runs, and forced a change over to the slower bowlers.

This was a real Comptonian innings. After hitting Goddard "round the corner" for another boundary the Middlesex batsman pranced several paces down-wicket to Tayfield and turned the ball delicately to fine leg for yet another boundary. It was an astonishing shot which in a lesser batsman might have been considered a fluke. But Compton meant to do just that. The 50 was passed, Compton added another 4 off Goddard and lunch arrived at 61 for two, Compton 38, May 21. It was a gorgeous piece of batting by both men.

Despite ringing of the changes in bowling each of the pair passed his half century after lunch. Compton won the race to arrive there first, May being ten behind him. Compton had batted eighty minutes; May took 100 to his 50. It was too good to last. When the stand was worth 126 Compton was caught at first slip by Mansell, wide and hard off Heine. I enjoyed his 71 that day far more even than his 158 of the first innings. He was the batsman of ten years earlier, able and willing to tear any bowling to pieces.

When Compton was out May was 53. His next partner was Cowdrey, who after making 6 was missed in the slips by Mansell off Goddard. Cowdrey did not begin his innings very happily, but he improved as time went on. He and May stayed together until about half an hour before the close; then May was bowled by Mansell. He had made 117—his second century in successive Tests. If his runs were not achieved with quite the same brilliant unorthodoxy as Compton's, they were always produced elegantly and the power of his driving was prodigious.

In order to save Bailey's wicket for the morrow Lock was

sent in to join Cowdrey and there were no further casualties that day. Lock is a new and valuable discovery in Test batsmanship, showing an ability to "stay there" such as the late Hedley Verity displayed on many occasions, but Lock has more strokes than Verity possessed. That night he served his side well by holding the fort for half an hour. It was noteworthy that McGlew did not bring the new ball into action that night, although by the end of the day it was 50 runs overdue. Instead the slower bowlers, particularly Goddard and Tayfield, had to work overtime.

FIFTH DAY

England were all out for 381 and the South Africans,
scoring 145 for seven, won the match by three wickets.

Here indeed was a tight squeeze for the victors, for they could not round off their victory until five minutes before the time fixed for the end of the match. There were moments when South Africa seemed likely to win; when England looked like turning the tables, and when a draw appeared the probable outcome.

England were not all out until tea time, chiefly because Bailey stayed on in his patient way, and Evans made a better 36 with his injured hand than he can often make with a sound one.

Directly play was resumed the overdue new ball was taken by Heine and Adcock against the overnight not-outs, Cowdrey and Lock. With the old ball Heine appealed against Lock for a catch at the wicket, but Waite dropped the ball and the shout was stifled.

Cowdrey looked far from comfortable and took a rap on the fingers from Adcock which made him flick them in pain. It damaged his right hand, which he repeatedly withdrew from the bat in making his strokes. In three-quarters of an hour's batting Cowdrey scored only one run, while Lock increased his overnight three to 17. When the total was 270 and the day's play was nearly an hour old Lock tried to drive Adcock, and gave McGlew an easy catch at mid-on.

Enter Bailey. By then England were 33 runs ahead. Lock had held on during two days for an hour and twenty minutes, making 17 towards a stand of 36 with Cowdrey.

Cowdrey arrived at his 50 at last by hitting his first boundary of the day—a hook off Heine. He had been batting for four hours. Hardly had he completed his half-century than he was out, caught by Goddard at second slip. The fieldsman threw himself forward to take a very good catch close to the ground. Two hundred and seventy-four for six. Cowdrey's innings, while stubborn and courageous, was certainly not up to his best standard. He played like a batsman who was not seeing the ball properly.

Bailey and Titmus were still together at lunch time—293 for six or 56 ahead. Bailey had then been in for an hour and five minutes for 6, made in two scoring strokes, and Titmus fifty minutes for 10, made in three. After lunch Titmus, having hit two more boundaries, was caught in the slips off Adcock. With Tyson in Bailey opened out a bit. Tyson was bowled at 325 and Bedser, l.b.w. to Heine, at 333.

In this crisis Evans appeared with his broken finger, still in plaster, sticking through a cut-away hole in his batting glove. A characteristic innings of 36 from him followed and he and Trevor Bailey added 48 together. Evans hit seven fours during his stay of forty minutes, treating the bowling of Heine, Goddard and Tayfield with complete disdain. Often he withdrew his injured hand from the bat when making his defensive stroke, but his driving was necessarily a two-handed affair, and he found he could hit the ball hard enough in all conscience so long as he held his injured finger clear of the bat bandle. The crowd, worked up into a state of high excitement, were disappointed indeed when Evans was out. Facing Tayfield he sent a ball high between McLean and Heine, and McLean made the catch.

It was Evans's last public appearance of the season. The finger did not heal in time to allow him any more cricket that season. Bailey was thus left partnerless after batting nearly three hours for 38, made in successive stands with Cowdrey, Titmus, Tyson, Bedser and Evans, all of whom he survived.

Now could South Africa accomplish the task of making

145 runs to win in two and a quarter hours? They did accomplish it, yet how near were they to failure and England to victory. Under the regulations the tea and innings intervals were merged, and at a quarter past four McGlew and Goddard opened the South African venture.

To begin with it looked rather like a schoolboyish game of tip-and-run, for they scored 14 in two overs by running pretty nearly every time ball met bat. Graveney, who had bruised a hand in his former wicketkeeping, now stood so far back to Tyson that he could not gallop up to the wicket in time to receive the ball from the fieldsman. Lock turned himself into an extremely short-range mid-off and again combined with these duties those of taking over when necessary behind the stumps.

Goddard was first out at 18, after only ten minutes—caught by May in trying to drive Bedser. A few minutes later his successor, Keith, was bowled for a duck and two were out for 23. I wondered how soon, if at all, the South Africans would put up the shutters. Certainly McLean, their most dangerous forcing batsman, showed no signs of it. Among his early strokes was a six off Bedser, to whom a little later he gave a difficult chance of catching and bowling him.

McLean went on his merry way and in one thrilling minute or two hooked Tyson three times to the boundary. There seemed, with only an hour to go, and 95 runs on the board, that the South African task would become easy, but the visitors' cause had a violent set-back when McLean was run out. From one of his strokes his partner, McGlew, backed up too hard and Parkhouse threw in to the bowler's end after the batsmen had crossed over. McLean had scored exactly 50 and the partnership had been worth 72 in a few minutes under the hour. Ninety-five for three.

Winslow, that lovely hitter of sixes, succeeded McLean and twice lifted balls from Bedser over the boundary line before Tyson bowled him. One hundred and twelve for four. There was a slower period of scoring when McGlew and Mansell were in company, and then both these batsmen were out almost together—Mansell l.b.w. to Tyson and McGlew bowled by the same bowler, with the totals respectively 129 and 132.

By now only 13 runs were needed. After three of them had

been made Endean was caught in the slips by Titmus off Lock.
This brought together Waite and Tayfield. The winning hit
was made by Waite—a drive off Tyson for four which was not
the least majestic stroke of the many in this courageous South
African innings. Knowing well that they could not afford to
risk drawing this game they had gone out for the runs and had
risked defeat. I was glad that their enterprise had brought
victory. It had been a magnificent cricket match—all five days
of it. The high spots were two superb innings by Compton; the
courageous century of the much-battered McGlew, and the
hundreds later on of Waite and Winslow. Winslow's six-hit,
bringing him to his century, will long be discussed and described at Old Trafford.

The bowling honours had been shared out pretty evenly.
One man who had had less than his deserts was Lock, who had
bowled magnificently. Heine's five for 86 in the English
second innings, including the wickets of Kenyon, Compton and
Cowdrey, was another outstanding feat.

Complete scores are as follows:

ENGLAND

First Innings

D. Kenyon c Waite b Heine	5
T. W. Graveney c Tayfield b Adcock	0
P. B. H. May c Mansell b Goddard	34
D. C. S. Compton c Waite b Adcock	158
M. C. Cowdrey c Mansell b Tayfield	1
T. E. Bailey c Waite b Adcock	44
F. J. Titmus lbw b Heine	0
T. G. Evans c Keith b Heine	0
G. A. R. Lock not out	19
F. H. Tyson b Goddard	2
A. V. Bedser lbw b Goddard	1
Extras	20
Total	284

FALL OF WICKETS

1—2; 2—22; 3—70; 4—75; 5—219; 6—234; 7—242;
8—271; 9—280.

BOWLING

	O.	M.	R.	W.
Heine	24	4	71	3
Adcock	28	5	52	3
Tayfield	35	15	57	1
Goddard	27	10	52	3
Mansell	6	2	13	0
Keith	6	1	19	0

SOUTH AFRICA

FIRST INNINGS

D. J. McGlew not out	104
T. L. Goddard c Graveney b Tyson	62
H. J. Keith c Graveney b Bailey	38
P. N. F. Mansell lbw b Lock	7
W. R. Endean c Evans b Lock	5
R. A. McLean b Tyson	3
J. H. B. Waite c Kenyon b Bedser	113
P. L. Winslow lbw b Bedser	108
H. J. Tayfield b Tyson	28
P. Heine not out	22
Extras	31

Total (8 wickets dec.) 521

N. A. T. Adcock did not bat.

FALL OF WICKETS

1—147; 2—171; 3—179; 4—182; 5—245; 6—416; 7—457;
8—494.

BOWLING

	O.	M.	R.	W.
Bedser	31	2	92	2
Tyson	44	5	124	3
Bailey	37	8	102	1
Lock	64	24	121	2
Titmus	19	7	51	0

ENGLAND

SECOND INNINGS

D. Kenyon c Waite b Heine	1
T. W. Graveney b Adcock	1
P. B. H. May b Mansell	117
D. C. S. Compton c Mansell b Heine	71
M. C. Cowdrey c Goddard b Heine	50
G. A. R. Lock c McGlew b Adcock	17
T. E. Bailey not out	38
F. J. Titmus c Mansell b Adcock	19
F. H. Tyson b Heine	8
A. V. Bedser c Waite b Heine	3
T. G. Evans c McLean b Tayfield	36
Extras	20
	—
Total	381

FALL OF WICKETS

1—2; 2—2; 3—126; 4—234; 5—270; 6—274; 7—304; 8—325; 9—333.

BOWLING

	O.	M.	R.	W.
Heine	32	8	86	5
Adcock	28	12	48	3
Goddard	47	21	92	0
Tayfield	51·5	21	102	1
Mansell	15	3	33	1

SOUTH AFRICA

Second Innings

D. J. McGlew b Tyson	..	..	..	..	48
T. L. Goddard c May b Bedser		..	..		8
H. J. Keith b Bedser	..	..	..	..	0
R. A. McLean run out	..	..	..	..	50
P. L. Winslow b Tyson	..	..	..	..	16
P. N. F. Mansell lbw b Tyson	..	..	..		4
J. H. B. Waite not out	..	..	..	..	10
W. R. Endean c Titmus b Lock	..	..	..		2
H. J. Tayfield not out	..	..	..	..	1
Extras ..	..	..	..	..	6

Total (7 wickets)   145

P. Heine and N. A. T. Adcock did not bat.

Fall of Wickets

1—18; 2—23; 3—95; 4—112; 5—129; 6—132; 7—135.

Bowling

	O.	M.	R.	W.
Tyson	.. .. 13·3	2	55	3
Bedser	 10	1	61	2
Lock	 7	2	23	1

South Africa won by 3 wickets.

CHAPTER IX

THE CHAMPIONS BEATEN

IN cricket the victories and defeats of one match are obscured by those of the next. Hardly had the Test Match at Manchester been lost than the Englishmen had to go tearing back to Lord's to take part in Gentlemen *v.* Players. On the other hand the South Africans were lucky in having the only three-day break in a tour lasting from early May to the middle of September. Even so they did not permit themselves much of a holiday, for they were back in London for practice the day before their next match, against Surrey at the Oval.

Why, I wonder, do the programme planners insist on planting a match like Gentlemen *v.* Players right into the middle of the Test Match series? This time most of the interest in the game was destroyed because several Test players on both sides had to withdraw through injuries. Some of my fellow-writers would like to see this venerable fixture scrapped altogether, on the ground that the match nowadays has little meaning. I do not agree with them, if only because these representative games raise the standard of English cricket by bringing the best players together. There ought to be more, rather than fewer, of such fixtures, but Gentlemen *v.* Players should be taken away from the late June to middle August period during which the Tests are being played at fortnightly intervals. The match could be used in early June as an England trial game, or be deferred until late August or early September. Such a fixture near the end of the season would be a fitting climax to the domestic programme.

As with the game against Yorkshire, so with that against Surrey, the South Africans were facing opposition strong enough to provide a sort of extra Test Match. The County side contained six men who had played for England—May, Barrington, McIntyre, Laker, Loader and A. V. Bedser. Unfortunately the County put up rather a poor show. The South Africans, captained by Endean because both Cheetham and McGlew were injured, scored 244 in their first innings, chiefly because of the brilliant 151 by McLean. It was not a commanding score in the circumstances, but Surrey were all out to Goddard, Fuller, Tayfield and Mansell for 140. The only batsmen to reach double figures were May 62 and Constable 34.

The South African second innings was almost as poor. Laker taking five for 56 on a rain-affected wicket. The total was only 170 and Surrey were set with 275 to make to win. Clark, Stewart and May gave the venture a good start, and later Barrington played a useful innings, but the down-the-list batsmen failed and all were out for 192 so that the South Africans won by 82 runs. Tayfield was the destroyer on this occasion—eight for 76.

The Queen always likes to have presented to her members of touring sides from overseas. Usually her visits are made to Lord's, but this time she went to the Oval for the first time in her life on the Monday of this match. Unfortunately the Duke of Edinburgh, who is an ardent cricket follower and a useful player, was unable to accompany her, but the Queen, who watched the play from the Committee Room in the pavilion, had the proceedings explained to her by Lord Tedder, President of Surrey, and by Sir John Hobbs. She arrived in the late afternoon, remained to tea, chatted with the players of both sides who were presented to her on the grass in front of the pavilion, and watched the game for about an hour.

So heavy were the inroads made by injuries to the English side that the selectors delayed from Sunday to Monday their announcement of the eleven for the Fourth Test Match at Leeds. Willie Watson, of Yorkshire, was a certainty for a place, but ironically he was struck on the arm at Lord's by a ball while batting for his County against Middlesex at the very time the selectors were at work.

Lord's on that day had a sort of parade of "hospital cases" to ascertain who could and who could not play. Tyson, who had strained an ankle in the Manchester match and who had a body strain as well, failed to pass the test of fitness and so had to stand down from the match. So had Cowdrey. There were in all six changes in the English side, though not all of them were dictated by injury. Lowson, of Yorkshire, came in as opening batsman in place of Kenyon. Insole, the Essex captain, was included instead of Cowdrey who had missed the Gentlemen *v.* Players match in the vain hope that his injured hand would recover in time. McIntyre, of Surrey, kept wicket instead of Evans, Statham was able to resume his place, Loader displaced Bedser. The selectors, abandoning all ideas of playing an off-spinner, reintroduced Wardle, in addition to playing Lock, so there were two slow left-handers.

This was Loader's second Test Match, his first being against Pakistan at the Oval the previous season. Insole, who had shown outstanding form for his County, had had only one Test before—against the West Indies at Nottingham in 1950.

The team was therefore as follows: Lowson, Bailey, May, Lock, Compton, Graveney, Insole, McIntyre, Wardle, Statham, Loader. This was the batting order in the first innings; it was altered in the second, when Bailey and Lock dropped down to their customary places in the list.

The South Africans, in their usual mysterious way, announced thirteen names in Leeds on the afternoon before the match, adding Fuller and Duckworth to the eleven who had won at Manchester. Everyone believed, however, that with the captain, Cheetham, still carrying his arm in a sling, the victors of Old Trafford would take the field at Headingley unchanged, and so it proved.

CHAPTER X

THE FOURTH TEST MATCH

*Played at Headingley, Leeds, on 21st, 22nd, 23rd, 25th,
26th July, and won by South Africa by 224 runs at
tea-time on the fifth day.*

FIRST DAY

*South Africa were all out for 171 in the first innings
and England lost two wickets for 25.*

IT was an astonishing innings which the South Africans
played in opening this Test Match of fluctuating fortunes.
They won the toss for the first time in the series, decided to bat
as a matter of course, and in an hour and twenty minutes
scored 33 without loss. Yet seven men were out for 98 on a
perfect batting wicket, and though there was a late recovery
the whole side were out for a paltry total. True, our batsmen
emulated theirs in mediocrity, but that story belongs chiefly
to the second day's play.

The weather was fine and warm, though overcast, and the
ground looked as though no rain had fallen in Leeds for
months. There were big patches of brown at frequent intervals,
but the middle was green enough. The Englishmen, entering
the field through the lane of hero-worshippers tolerated at
Leeds, had first to tackle the stubborn South African openers
McGlew and Goddard—the one short and right-handed, the
other tall and left-handed. Our bowlers were the two 25-year-
old fast men Statham, now a Test veteran, and Loader of much
slighter experience.

McGlew, looking quite happy, was moderately brisk at the
start. He took a single off Statham's first over, a three off
Loader's first, and two twos off Statham's second. All this
happened before his partner had broken his duck. Even

Statham had a field more defensive than one usually sees from a fast bowler at the beginning of a Test Match. He had Wardle and Loader in the deep behind the bat, only two slips, Graveney and Insole, May in the gully and two short legs, Lowson and Lock.

Goddard did not score for a quarter of an hour, then he took a boundary off-driven from Loader. On this very ground Bradman once scored a triple century in a day in a Test Match against England. So little impression did our bowlers now appear to be making that one feared a tall total by the South Africans.

When Goddard was six and the total 18 he appeared from the ringside to be missed off two successive balls from Statham. The first stroke went to May in the gully, the second to Graveney in the slips. So fast were these balls travelling that it was difficult to see whether they went to earth before they reached the fieldsmen. I was told later by a closer witness than myself that a catch by May, though difficult, would have been physically possible but that the ball to Graveney fell short.

The first burst by our fast bowlers failed, Bailey was introduced to the bowling and Loader was transferred to Statham's end. Then at long last came success. Loader bowled to McGlew, who played forward in defence near the off-stump. Maybe the ball swung away from him. At any rate he touched it to the wicketkeeper. Thirty-three for one wicket, and the Englishmen must have felt pleased that McGlew had gone for as cheaply as 23 runs.

By now Goddard, plodding along, was eight runs rich in an hour and twenty minutes, and he was joined by a fellow left-hander in Keith. Keith did not score. With the total unchanged at 33 he flicked at a ball from Loader passing him on the leg side and again McIntyre held the catch, taken near his feet. Now Loader had bowled nine overs for nine runs and two wickets. In his later successful spell he had two wickets for one run in five overs.

The total advanced by only one run when Bailey came into the reckoning. The newcomer, Mansell, tried to break his duck by cutting him and turned the ball into his stumps.

Next came McLean, who was destined to give trouble.

Goddard, after staying in for an hour and three-quarters without reaching double figures, had his leg-stump knocked back by the irresistible Loader. Thirty-four for four.

Run-outs always seem to come at times of disaster like this. Just after lunch, with the total 38, Waite suffered in this manner. He played a ball from Bailey gently to backward point and began an optimistic run. McLean was not having any and Waite about-turned. The throw-in by Wardle to McIntyre beat him and he was out for two.

McLean, now joined by Winslow, rather tarnished Loader's figures by hitting him for two fours in one over, the second off a no-ball. The 50 came up at last and Winslow off-drove Loader for another four.

With the total 63 Winslow was bowled by Statham. McLean, now partnered by Endean, who in the beginning of his innings looked very unsure, struggled to save something from the wreck. He was deprived of four runs when a hook from Statham's bowling, travelling at tremendous speed, was "fielded" by umpire Chester, who took the ball full on the leg. Players ran up to offer their help, but although Chester must have been hurt, he refused to allow play to be interrupted.

The stand was broken after it had lasted about an hour by the dismissal of McLean. Loader, brought back for another spell, was the bowler and May made a splendid catch at cover-point, off his first ball. May had to make some ground to take the catch, which he secured about a foot from the ground. This meant 98 for seven.

The partnership which followed between Endean and Tayfield was the swiftest of the day. It added 56 before Statham bowled Endean. The tail-enders, Tayfield and Heine, had a useful little stand. Then Heine was bowled by Lock at 170 and a run later Adcock was l.b.w. to Statham. To describe Tayfield as a "tail-ender" is not altogether fair. His 25 not out was one of several good efforts with the bat.

England had an hour and ten minutes' batting and lost in that time the wickets of both openers, Bailey and Lowson, for 25 runs. The beginning was brisk beyond the ordinary, for Bailey hit a two and a four off the first two balls of Heine's opening over. That was too good to last, and the pair settled

down to defend until Bailey was l.b.w. to Heine with the total
15.

May drove the first ball he received from Heine to the
boundary. Near the end of the day Lowson, who had scored five
runs in about fifty-five minutes, was l.b.w. to Goddard; he
made no attempt at a stroke in the apparent belief that the
ball would miss the stumps. Twenty-three for two.

Lock joined May and the two played out time. Just before
the end Adcock limped off the field. No one thought then that
his part in the match was over except for a brief appearance
with the bat; but so it was. He told me that evening that he had
twisted his foot in a hole dug by various fast bowlers in their
run-up. The injury was to the base of the second toe of his
left foot, and an X-ray showed a fracture in a small bone whose
medical description I am too ignorant to remember.

Chief honours of the day from England's point of view had
gone to Statham and Loader. Loader, four for 52, had special
reason for pride, since his bag included four of the first five
batsmen, McGlew, Goddard, Keith and McLean.

SECOND DAY

*England were all out for 191—a lead of 20. In reply
South Africa made 107 for no wicket in the second
innings.*

This certainly was South Africa's day. Ours was a disappointing, almost insignificant, first innings lead and the two
South African openers, McGlew and Goddard, took their side
by evening 87 runs ahead almost untroubled. Our batsmen,
who certainly did not distinguish themselves, had to struggle
hard to gain their modest advantage; it would not have been
theirs at all had it not been for some out-and-out hitting by
Johnny Wardle.

When McGlew led his men into the field Adcock was
missing, and Fuller fielded as twelfth man. A very fine fieldsman
he is. For a while all went well with the overnight not-outs,

Keith going down on one knee (*above*) almost plays a ball on to his wicket off Wardle

FOURTH

TEST

asole is dropped the slips off Heine (*above*)

ompton (*right*) ives low in an fort to hold a ifficult catch by ndean off Statham

Heine hears the "death rattle" (*left*) as a ball from Bailey curls past his bat

Bailey is caught and bowled by
Tayfield (*top*) during England's
second innings at Leeds

Doug' Insole also loses his wicket
to a catch in the same innings
(*centre*)—this time by Keith.
Goddard is the bowler

The South African team are
clapped and cheered off the field
(*left*) after their fine victory in
the fourth Test Match

May 7 and Lock 2. Stop-gap or nightwatchman—call him what you will—Lock certainly did not bat like a man who felt his job was over. The on-drive he soon took off Goddard for three was one which would have done credit to May himself. May for his part hit two boundaries off Heine.

When the total was 51 and May had made 18 there came an appeal unnecessarily raucous for a catch at the wicket off Heine. Umpire Chester rejected it. But just afterwards the other umpire Bartley answered more favourably another appeal—for l.b.w. against Lock to Goddard's bowling. Lock's batting has developed. There is no reason now why this determined cricketer should not become an all-rounder in the fullest sense—bowling, fielding and batting. A season or two ago he went in number eleven for Surrey, and even then looked the best last man in England. In this innings his 17 runs were worth quite a lot.

Now that Lock had gone our main batsmen came together. Compton joined May, the England captain at that time being 20. They took the total from 53 to 117, and Compton raised the Goddard siege with a variety to attacking strokes, beginning with a sweep for four. May took boundaries off Goddard and Tayfield, but Compton made most of the running.

Ten minutes before lunch visions of a century partnership between them were dashed when May, playing forward to Tayfield, was bowled. He apparently edged the ball on to his stumps. Of the partnership of 64, Compton had made 36. May had batted in his best style for 47, scored during 35 minutes the previous day and an hour and 50 minutes up to nearly lunch time.

Compton and Graveney were together at lunch. The patient, untiring Goddard had come off a quarter of an hour before the interval after bowling 19 overs for 35 runs and Lock's wicket. The last runs before the break were a streaky four by Compton off Heine through the slips.

After lunch runs hardly existed for a while. One only came in the first three overs, bowled by Heine and Tayfield. There followed a four off Heine by Compton, bringing him to the verge of his 50. The first real attacking stroke of the afternoon was a four driven by Graveney off Heine. The batsman hit

G

the ball as easily and cleanly as he achieves a drive from the tee at golf.

Compton's half century arrived just afterwards—the fourth innings this series in which he had contributed this or something better. He had scored a run every two minutes.

Only too often something happens to Graveney just when one feels he is finding his feet. Now he tried to hook Heine, missed and was l.b.w. for 10. This all added up to 152 for five, or still 19 behind. Compton was now 61 and Insole his new partner.

Insole had not scored when Compton was out. He lobbed up a simple-looking catch off Tayfield to Mansell at short slip. It seemed that the ball went from bat to pad to fieldsman. Compton had batted eighty minutes for his 61, perhaps not as brilliantly as he had at Manchester, but still very soundly. His first chance was his last.

So it happened that the sixth-wicket pair, Insole and McIntyre, came into action with nothing on the scoreboard credited to either of them. It took Insole a quarter of an hour to get off the mark, and an anxious time he had both before and after this happened. It was very far from a happy innings of his, but he was destined to do better later in the match.

McIntyre broke his duck with a hit for two, but that stroke and a single were his only runs. With the total 161 Heine had him l.b.w. In half an hour wickets had now fallen at 152, 152, and 161.

Cliff Gladwin, of Derbyshire, is the hero of a famous cricket story of South African origin. Going in to bat in a Test Match crisis he reputedly remarked to a fieldsman on his way in, "Cometh the hour, cometh the man,"—and the match was won by running a leg-bye. Johnny Wardle, taking his part in this new crisis of 1955, might have said something equally resounding, but I don't think he did.

Anyhow he behaved as though he were indeed the man for the hour. For the first few minutes his batting was as cagey as Insole's own. Then, casting dull care aside, he proceeded to score 24 runs in six hits. The first of these, off Tayfield's bowling, scattered the spectators far behind the bowler. Next ball went for four. Two runs later he tried another six with a ball which I thought would forestall the space satellites of President Eisenhower.

McLean had an outside chance of catching it as it fell, but he could not hold on and the ball trickled over the boundary for another four. The lead had arrived.

In Tayfield's next over Wardle continued his good work. He hit him for a two, then another six, then another two—here he was missed by Goddard—and then tried another six. This proved his undoing, for Goddard held the catch.

Wardle went out in a thunder of Yorkshire applause, greater in volume than those for May and Compton combined. 186 for eight—a lead by now of 15. Statham entered, hit one rugged four and was bowled by Tayfield. Finally Insole was l.b.w., like five of the men out before him. The innings ended for 191.

The South African second innings, beginning at ten minutes to four, came before and after a belated tea interval. Twenty minutes after McGlew and Goddard began their long partnership the arrears were wiped off, and by tea-time McGlew had scored 24 runs and Goddard 18. Despite defensive bowling by Bailey the batsmen made such good progress that in two hours they scored 107 without being parted. Statham, Loader, Bailey, Wardle and Lock all bowled to them in vain. McGlew passed his 50 and Goddard ended only four short of it.

A thoroughly disappointing day, the turning point in the match.

THIRD DAY

South Africa advanced their score from 107 for no wicket to 341 for five.

This was a hot, hardworking, disheartening day for the Englishmen in the field. Not a wicket fell until the first ball of the afternoon when Wardle and McIntyre between them broke the opening stand of 176.

The day was the most brilliant one of a brilliant week.

Sydney, Melbourne or Brisbane could not surpass the white and gay-coloured shorts and frocks decorating the great ring of the Headingley ground.

McGlew, small, mercurial, determined, and Goddard, tall, rather stolid, and equally resolute, had made 107 together in two hours and twenty minutes the previous day. When they resumed their innings they were in no difficulties in opposition to Statham and Lock. The chief chance of a wicket to England indeed lay in a run-out. McGlew and Goddard tried various cheeky singles; one of them might have been fatal to Goddard if the return of Lowson from cover to the bowler, Statham, had been straight.

When McGlew was 66 a ball from Lock gave a distinct click as it passed the batsman. McIntyre, holding the ball, appealed for a catch, but umpire Chester did not attribute the noise to the impact of ball on bat.

After fifty minutes the 150 total arrived. All this while Lock was being economical at one end, while from the other the bowling was shared by Statham and Bailey. After Lock had bowled 11 overs for 22 runs Wardle gave him a rest. The Yorkshireman, running through his overs at Chris Chataway speed, bowled his first three without a run against him and the fourth contained only a single. With Bailey bowling defensively at the other end the scoring became very slow. Loader came into the attack at the "fast" end.

Goddard, when he had made 73, might have been caught by Graveney off Wardle in the slips but he did not get to the ball in time. Again Goddard was almost run out when scrambling a run from Wardle. This time May's throw was not gathered by McIntyre as he broke the wicket, but the ball reached the wicketkeeper very awkwardly.

At lunch-time the total was 176 for no wicket. But the first ball after the interval, bowled by Wardle, was touched by Goddard to the wicketkeeper. One hundred and seventy-six for one, McGlew 98 and one left-hander replaced by another, Keith. McGlew did not reach his hundred in the flamboyant manner of Winslow at Manchester. Loader beat and nearly bowled him after an anxious period, and then at last the century came from a three past point off the same bowler.

McGlew and Keith showed confidence against our two slow left-handers, Lock and Wardle, bowling together. The total stood at 198 when Lowson, fielding at slip to Wardle, let a lobbed ball from Keith fall to the ground. There was no need for that groan, for the ball had come off pad or clothing, not the bat.

The 200 total was duly passed, but May did not immediately take the new ball. Lock's spell of bowling went on until he was looking "dead beat". The fast bowlers were recalled and the new ball was brought into use at 223. For the first time Loader had the advantage of bowling down-wind.

Scoring was still sedate and now and then the heated crowd on the popular side broke into a slow handclap. The rate became rather less slow against the faster bowlers, but it was still much too leisurely for the liking of the crowd.

At tea the total had gone up to 258 for one; in other words only 82 had been scored in just over two hours since lunch. Ten minutes after tea McGlew was out. He was caught at mid-wicket by May off Wardle's bowling. His score, which included thirteen fours, was 133 out of 265 then on the board. He and Keith had added 89 together, and he had batted for six and three-quarter hours. I cannot pretend that it was an effervescent innings, but it was the foundation for the South African victory.

In came McLean at a moment when he might surely have been expected to make many a hearty run against the tired bowling. In fact he made only three. Then, trying to hit Wardle, he was caught by Lowson. He pulled the ball fiercely to the fieldsman, standing fairly close in, who doubled up and a moment afterwards we discovered that the ball had found a resting place in his midriff. Only the fieldsman himself can say what degrees of luck and skill there were about that catch. Two hundred and sixty-nine for three.

Winslow came next in a stand of 34 with Keith. During most of this partnership Statham and Wardle were the bowlers. Keith at last became tired of being tied up by Wardle, tried a huge hit and was bowled. England's position was improving. Eight runs later Winslow was well caught by Lock off Statham. He tried a hook and the fieldsman had an awkward run and a difficult judgment to make in securing the ball. That was the last wicket to fall on this third day of the game. Endean and Waite remained together to the end, despite some attacking bowling by Lock and Wardle.

Bad though the day had been for England it looked right up to lunch time as though it would be much worse.

FOURTH DAY

South Africa were all out in the second innings for exactly 500 and England were set to make 481 runs to win the match. At the close they had scored 115 for two wickets.

Though this was a Monday all gates of the Headingley ground had to be closed. I had been told that accommodation was available for 40,000 but in fact the attendance was about 4000 short of this number. Various West Riding towns, including Sheffield, were having a works holiday and incoming trains were packed.

The day began as solemnly as though this were the opening morning with a blank score-board, a new ball and fresh fast bowlers. Wardle bowled two maiden overs to Waite and Loader one to Endean before a run was scored. Then Loader conceded a single to Endean and Wardle bowled his third maiden to that batsman for a change. A quarter of an hour passed with only one scored, but thereafter runs came more freely. Endean hit two boundaries in one over from Wardle, the first a square cut, the second a hook off one of the bowler's rare long hops.

The crowd badly wanted elbow room. The game indeed was held up while numbers overflowed on to the grass behind the bowler's arm. They were moved by the joint efforts of Chester and a policeman, but presently returned in larger numbers and perforce were allowed to remain seated on the grass. Headingley is a very efficiently run ground, but this business of spectators behind the bowler's arm will need attention before the Australians go there next year.

The first hour yielded 41 runs, which, considering the quiet opening, was quite a fair rate of progress. Lock had gone in for Wardle and Bailey for Loader. At 387, after a stand of 76 by Endean and Waite, a wicket fell. McIntyre, keeping wicket to Lock, tried to stump Waite; it seemed a close thing but the appeal was refused. It did not matter, for the next ball was caught by McIntyre from a snick by the same batsman.

With Mansell in we feared another English casualty when Peter May, running full tilt to try to cut off a drive by Endean, disappeared among the crowd in much the same way as did Jean Borotra in the old days of his leaps and tumbles at Wimbledon. May was tripped up by a low wire-netting fence erected to prevent waste paper from drifting over the field in the breeze. He vanished among a group of boys sitting on the grass, but reappeared unhurt except that he had barked an elbow. This boundary, and another which followed in the same over, completed Endean's 50.

Just as the 400 total was signalled Mansell, after scoring one run towards a stand of 13 with Endean, was l.b.w. to Bailey.

Statham came on for the first time that day at 408, although as the second new ball of the innings had not been taken until 223, the third was not yet falling due. At lunch time only two wickets had fallen that day, and the score stood at 418 for seven—Endean 61, his highest of the series, and Tayfield 6.

Soon after lunch it became certain we should have to score more than 400 runs to win. Our highest *winning* fourth innings total had been 332 for seven against Australia at Melbourne in 1928–9. We drew what comfort we could from the recollection that in 1948 the Australians, batting on this very ground of Headingley, scored 404 for three and beat us.

The new ball was taken directly it was due, but without immediate results; when it was ceasing to be new Tayfield was l.b.w. to Statham after a stand of 39 with Endean.

Heine stayed in long enough for Endean to reach his nineties—92 to be exact—and then was bowled by Bailey. Four hundred and sixty-eight for nine—and the crowd, knowing of Adcock's injury, probably assumed that the innings was over. Not a bit of it. McGlew, as captain, was anxious to squeeze every possible run and Adcock appeared. He was without a runner and made much better progress on a foot in plaster than had seemed possible. He usually wears two or three pairs of socks under his boot, which was thus big enough to go on over the plaster.

Endean kept the bowling as much as he could, but Adcock was far from helpless when facing it and could run quite well on the heel of his injured foot. Endean, hooking a four off Wardle, completed his century—his first against England, though he scored one in Australia and another in New Zealand in Test Matches there. He had hit thirteen fours and had batted three hours and fifty minutes.

Adcock was batting better, indeed, with a bad foot than he often does with a good one. He hit a boundary on his own account. Endean, now using his strokes freely, took three fours off Bailey in two overs and brought up the 500, at which point Adcock was bowled by Bailey. Endean was left not out with 116.

The English second innings began at 3.50, and began very badly. A bye and a two hit by Graveney were the only runs before Lowson was out for a duck. He played back to a ball from Goddard and touched it into his wicket. This time the second member, Graveney, of the English opening pair did better. He and May were together for seventy minutes, before and after tea, for 56 runs. Graveney was severe on Tayfield. Yet one is always fearful, when Graveney's strokes are flowing freely, that something untoward may soon happen. In this case Graveney tried to hit Tayfield once too often, and was very well caught low down by McLean at mid-off. Fifty-nine for two.

Compton's knee, the one that troubles him intermittently, was rather sore and puffy after all the running about he had done, and he wanted, if possible, to rest it until the morrow, so his place at number four was filled by Insole with satisfactory results. He and May remained together for the rest of the day, adding 56. It was a different Insole from the faltering batsman of the first innings; indeed, his 30 not out at the end of the day showed he had scored faster than his captain. The only semblance of a chance given by these partners was a hook by May which sent the ball short of the twelfth man, Fuller. The fieldsman made all the ground he could, but could not make enough to secure the catch. So at the end of the day, 115 for two, we still needed 366 for victory.

FIFTH DAY

England were all out for 256 and South Africa won by 224 runs at 4.10 p.m.

It was a tall order our batsmen faced on this last day of the match—an order which, despite the morning optimism, they were unable to implement. Soon after May, 47, and Insole, 30, came to the middle to resume their innings Heine, the only fast bowler South Africa had in action, tested his run-up. Apparently he did not like the foothold, which was pitted, and he gave way to the slower Goddard, left-handed and medium-paced.

Off the first ball of the day May, with a square cut, reduced the deficit from 365 to 361 and reached his own half-century. This was his fourth score in this series of 50 or more, including two centuries.

From the other end Mansell, the leg-spinner who had not been bowled very much in Test Matches, began a long spell. Runs were rare, largely because the South African ground fielding was so alert and agile. No matter how hard the batsmen banged the ball there always seemed to be a South African in the way. McGlew, in particular, was always willing to throw himself flat and full length on the hard ground to turn fours into singles.

Insole's touch, uncertain at the day's beginning, grew firm. May's was never anything else. In half an hour the score had advanced by 16. Occasionally a boundary came from May, and the third of them that morning brought up the 150. There seemed a suspicion of "edge" about the stroke, which went through the slips off Goddard's bowling.

After an hour and ten minutes the 100 partnership, begun the previous day, was completed; 56 of these runs had been made overnight. The partners had been together just over two hours and May's scoring rate had been only slightly higher than Insole's.

We were just wondering when McGlew intended to try another bowler when Goddard took the wicket of Insole. He was caught neatly by Keith at fine leg after making 47 towards a stand of 101. One hundred and sixty for three.

Denis Compton joined May and immediately hit Mansell through the covers for four by way of breaking his duck. May followed up with a boundary off-driven from Goddard. Compton brought into play that short-armed hook of his. It would have carried over the boundary but for the fleetness of Fuller, and that tired knee of Compton's had to stand the strain of running three.

It was not until an hour and a half after the day's cricket began that the first bowling change was made by the acting captain. Tayfield replaced Mansell, but Goddard, able and willing to bowl till the cows come home, continued from the other end. The tall well-built Goddard adds a wonderful physique to his skill as batsman and bowler. May presently achieved his sweetest stroke of the morning—a square cut off Tayfield streaking the ball to the boundary. He was batting exquisitely, and Compton had settled down well.

May brought up the 200 with his only streaky stroke of the morning—a snick off Goddard which carried the ball through the air just wide of slip. It went for four runs. In the last over before lunch came a blow from which England never recovered. May, facing Tayfield, played defensively forward and was l.b.w. to him. May was deprived of his century—he made 97—and England of her mainstay in batting. The total was 204 for four, Compton then 20. May had batted for three and a half hours, with 13 fours, and was applauded all the way to the pavilion.

Lunch was taken immediately after May's dismissal. He had every reason to be proud of his series of innings during his first season as captain of England; so far his contributions were: 83, 0, 112, 34, 117, 47, and now 97. Two more balls would have taken him undefeated in to lunch, for he was out to the fourth ball of Tayfield's over.

Goddard, who had bowled all morning for 22 overs, 37 runs and a wicket, resumed with Tayfield immediately after lunch. Compton's new partner was Bailey, whose dogged, never-say-die personality might well have been daunted at the prospect of battling on for the rest of the day in the hope of a draw. Chances of a win had faded almost to nothingness. Compton, hitting Goddard hard round to leg, gave a technical chance. The fieldsman, Endean, jumping high, got one hand to the ball, but it brushed over his fingers and went for a single. Bailey seemed content to sport his impregnable barndoor.

The downfall of Compton extinguished all hope of a favourable result for England. Facing Goddard, he advanced his bat at a ball over the off-stump in an attempt at an attacking stroke, but was caught behind the wicket. Two hundred and ten for five, Bailey no score yet. Compton had batted 70 minutes for his 26.

McIntyre entered, but did not stay long. He did see, at close quarters, Bailey take his first single after being in for 20 minutes, but with the total 215 McIntyre tried to hook Tayfield and Heine caught him at mid wicket.

I could not understand the English tactics during this period. At one end Bailey was defending with his customary stoutheartedness, at the other batsmen were going out to attacking strokes when there was no chance whatever of winning the match. Conceivably there might have been a chance of drawing it if more restrained methods had been adopted.

Wardle was cheered to the wicket by the Yorkshire crowd as though capable of winning the game off his own bat. He hit Tayfield for a couple of early fours while Bailey defended dourly. Then, in his next over from Tayfield, Wardle slammed a six—the ball was just too high for Fuller to capture.

Round Bailey fieldsmen clustered like flies round a jampot; but he is a real dead-bat expert and ball after ball was played firmly down to earth right under the batsman's nose. Wardle met his inevitable fate, lifting a catch to Heine at coverpoint off Tayfield. Two hundred and thirty-nine for seven, Wardle 21 and Bailey still only one single in 50 minutes.

Lock came in with altogether different intentions. Obviously his idea was to emulate Bailey. Minute after minute went by without a run. Runs, indeed, no longer mattered. When Lock did take a single there were uproarious cheers. The drinks were brought out; both batsmen were total abstainers.

Lock, having scored three in 23 minutes while his partner clung to his beloved single, was hit on the foot by Goddard, winced, but carried on.

This attempt to put up the shutters came to an end after 40 minutes, during which seven runs had been made, all by Lock. That batsman was caught in the slips by Mansell off Goddard. Two hundred and forty-six for eight. Enter Statham. Bailey after batting nearly an hour and three quarters for his precious run added four more to it by driving Goddard to the boundary. Cheers.

Statham stayed with Bailey for half an hour before hitting his wicket. Two hundred and fifty-six for nine. Loader, the last man, came in and just afterwards Bailey, realising that the game was up, hit out at Tayfield and gave him a caught-and-bowled. Bailey had gone to the wicket immediately after lunch and had stayed there until the match ended at 4.10 p.m. for eight runs. We were beaten with more than two hours of playing time to spare.

Whether the match could have been drawn is a question to which no firm answer can be given. Bailey at least seemed of the opinion that such was possible. On the South African side the outstanding bowling performance was that of Goddard, who remained in action unrested right through the day. His figures were 46—27—45—4, his wickets that day included Insole, Compton, Lock and Statham. The previous evening he had bowled Lowson and during the whole innings he had taken five for 69.

Tayfield had taken one of the two wickets which mattered most, that of May, and he, too, ended the innings with five wickets, for 94 runs. The South Africans had triumphed despite the absence of their fast bowler, Adcock. They were cheered into the pavilion by a crowd big for the last day of the match, and there was the usual long wait for speeches which were never uttered.

The scores are as follows:

SOUTH AFRICA

FIRST INNINGS

D. J. McGlew c McIntyre b Loader	.. ..	23
T. L. Goddard b Loader	.. ..	9
H. J. Keith c McIntyre b Loader ..	.. ..	0
P. N. F. Mansell b Bailey ..	.. ..	0
R. A. McLean c May b Loader	.. ..	41
J. H. B. Waite run out ..	.. ..	2
P. L. Winslow b Statham ..	.. ..	8
W. R. Endean b Statham ..	.. ..	41
H. J. Tayfield not out ..	.. ..	25
P. S. Heine b Lock	.. ..	14
N. A. T. Adcock lbw b Statham	.. ..	8
Extras	.. ..	8
		—
Total	.. ..	171

FALL OF WICKETS

1—33; 2—33; 3—34; 4—34; 5—38; 6—83; 7—98; 8—154; 9—170.

BOWLING

	O.	M.	R.	W.
Statham	20·2	7	35	3
Loader	19	7	52	4
Bailey	16	7	23	1
Wardle	9	1	33	0
Lock	6	1	20	1

ENGLAND

FIRST INNINGS

T. E. Bailey lbw b Heine	9
F. A. Lowson lbw b Goddard	5
P. B. H. May b Tayfield	47
G. A. R. Lock lbw b Goddard	17
D. C. S. Compton c Mansell b Tayfield	61
T. W. Graveney lbw b Heine	10
D. J. Insole lbw b Heine	3
A. J. McIntyre lbw b Heine	3
J. H. Wardle c Goddard b Tayfield	24
J. B. Statham b Tayfield	4
P. J. Loader not out	0
Extras	8
Total	191

FALL OF WICKETS

1—15; 2—23; 3—53; 4—117; 5—152; 6—152; 7—161; 8—186; 9—191.

BOWLING

	O.	M.	R.	W.
Heine	29·5	11	70	4
Adcock	4	3	4	0
Goddard	25	12	39	2
Tayfield	31	14	70	4

SOUTH AFRICA

SECOND INNINGS

D. J. McGlew c May b Wardle	133
T. L. Goddard c McIntyre b Wardle	74
H. J. Keith b Wardle	73
R. A. McLean c Lowson b Wardle	3
P. L. Winslow c Lock b Statham	19
W. R. Endean not out	116
J. H. B. Waite c McIntyre b Lock	32
P. N. F. Mansell lbw b Bailey	1
H. J. Tayfield lbw b Statham	14
P. S. Heine b Bailey	10
N. A. T. Adcock b Bailey	6
Extras	19
Total	500

FALL OF WICKETS

1—176; 2—265; 3—269; 4—303; 5—311; 6—387; 7—400; 8—439; 9—468.

BOWLING

	O.	M.	R.	W.
Statham	40	10	129	2
Loader	29	9	67	0
Bailey	40·5	11	97	3
Wardle	57	22	100	4
Lock	32	13	88	1

ENGLAND

SECOND INNINGS

F. A. Lowson b Goddard	0
T. E. Graveney c McLean b Tayfield	36
P. B. H. May lbw b Tayfield	97
D. J. Insole c Keith b Goddard	47
D. C. S. Compton c Waite b Goddard	26
T. E. Bailey c and b Tayfield	8
A. J. McIntyre c Heine b Tayfield	4
J. H. Wardle c Heine b Tayfield	21
G. A. R. Lock c Mansell b Goddard	7
J. B. Statham hit wkt b Goddard	3
P. J. Loader not out	0
Extras	7
	——
Total	256

FALL OF WICKETS

1—3; 2—59; 3—160; 4—204; 5—210; 6—215; 7—239; 8—246; 9—256.

BOWLING

	O.	M.	R.	W.
Heine	14	2	33	0
Goddard	62	37	69	5
Tayfield	47·1	15	94	5
Mansell	19	2	53	0

CHAPTER XI

AND NOW THE CLIMAX

"HEAVEN gie us a guid conceit o' ourselves," said some Scotsman, some time or other. Perhaps I ought to know who, but I don't. In cricketing matters we had certainly acquired that guid conceit in the last year or two. Had we not beaten Australia twice? The drawn series against Pakistan was an unfortunate slip, but nothing worse; and in the year of grace 1955 we had begun with two resounding victories over South Africa. Were the remaining Tests really worth playing? It hardly seemed so.

Our newspapers were not guiltless of slighting references to our opponents' abilities, though they were not so scathing as those of Australia were in the weeks before the Union men struck a blow at Commonwealth pride. The public still insisted on buying reserved seats in satisfying numbers for the remaining three matches, but then anything labelled "Test Match" in these days is liable to delude people into thinking they will inevitably see something wonderful. From a playing point of view the tour of the South Africans had promised to become nothing better than a flop.

Isaac Newton, I seem to remember from school days, once laid down that "action and reaction are equal and opposite". Certainly it applied to this astonishing series of Test Matches. England had won at Nottingham by an innings and five; at Lord's by 71. Then the staggering reaction. South Africa won at Manchester by three wickets, at Leeds by an out-and-out 224 runs, the sort of margin that Bradman, in his heyday, and his men used to inflict against us on behalf of Australia. Our pride and self-confidence were shaken.

No wonder that every seat at Kennington Oval was sold for the first three days of the match long in advance. People were not so optimistic about the fourth because in these times the Oval, fortunately, is not the batsman's paradise of pre-war days. No longer does it enable Len Hutton or anyone else to score innings of 364 runs.

The South African Test Match of four years previously, it was remembered, had taken no more than the time allotted to an ordinary County game. England won by four wickets in three days. Incidentally the only players who played in that game in 1951 and who had taken part, thus far, in any of the 1955 Tests were May, Lowson, Compton, and Bedser on the English side; and Endean, Cheetham, McLean and Mansell on the South African. Watson, who played in 1951, was also very much in the running in the present series, but injury kept him out of the fourth Test. He played only in the fifth.

The English Selectors had long and anxious deliberations during the days before the match. On the Monday at Kennington Oval, during the Surrey *v.* Middlesex game, we newspaper men were invited into the Secretary's office to hear the result from the Chairman of Selectors, G. O. Allen. This was the eleven, as chosen, in alphabetical order: Close, Compton, Cowdrey, Ikin, Laker, Lock, May (captain), Spooner, Statham, Tyson, Watson.

Why no Evans? His finger, broken at Manchester, had not sufficiently healed and the doctor told him he ought to play no more cricket that season. And why no Appleyard? His right shoulder had developed serious injury and he, too, was laid idle for the closing weeks of the summer. Here was a grievous handicap for the Selectors.

The side as chosen showed no fewer than seven changes from the one defeated at Leeds. Bailey, Graveney, Insole, Lowson, Loader, McIntyre and Wardle were all dropped—in McIntyre's case through injury. Five of the eleven newly selected, Ikin, Watson, Close, Spooner and Laker, were new to this series of Tests, though all of them had represented England in the past, and Watson would have played in the previous Test at Leeds had he been fit. It was noteworthy that five batsmen in this side were left-handers—Ikin, Watson, Close, Spooner and Statham. It needed no great insight into cricket to discern that this was an answer by the Selectors to the problem of Goddard, the South African left-hander whose leg-stump attack had been tying up our batsmen in previous matches. The only question was whether, with a great off-breaker like Tayfield in opposition, we were not leaping out of the frying-pan into the fire. To a left-hander Tayfield becomes a leg-spin bowler.

What of the men newly returned to the fray? Jack Ikin, 37 years of age, had played in 17 Test Matches against five different cricketing nations, his last appearance being against India in 1952. The Selectors were swayed not only by his "left-handedness" but by a burst of form for his County, Lancashire.

Close's experience of Test Match cricket had been slight and peculiar. In 1949, when chosen against New Zealand at the age of 18, he became the youngest Englishman ever picked to represent his country. He went to Australia in the 1950–1 tour, played in only one Test Match there and, quite candidly, was far from a success. That tour kept him away from Test Match cricket for more than four years, though his natural ability was obvious. He had great cricket in him, but it was slow in coming out.

His experiences for Yorkshire in 1955 had been unusual. Early in the season he lost his place in the County side for a short while, and then came back in a blaze of glory with a series of fine batting and bowling performances. In an emergency he had taken on the job of opening batsman for Yorkshire and a great success he had made of it. Surely it must be unique for a man to be dropped by his County and chosen to play for his country in the same season.

Spooner, the Warwickshire wicketkeeper, had had two tours with M.C.C. sides, one to India and one to the West Indies, and his Test experience had been limited to six matches out of this country. When his selection was announced the Chairman of Selectors said that, though McIntyre's injured hand had improved, the risk of playing him was not a justifiable one. Therefore Spooner had the place.

Laker, of course, is known as a frequent player of Test Matches, who has been either in the England side or on the fringe of it as an off-break bowler for many years. He had played 23 Tests for England against various countries. He and Lock between them won the Ashes for us in one afternoon at the Oval in 1953.

Back in 1950 he blew the England *v.* Rest Test Trial at
Bradford sky-high by taking for England eight wickets for
two runs, which my "Playfair" assures me is, statistically, the
finest figures ever recorded in first-class cricket. So I should
think.

Watson had played in 14 Tests. He scored 109 at Lord's
in the first one he played against Australia in 1953; and 116
at Kingston, Jamaica, in his first against West Indies, also
in 1953.

Note the chopping and changing in the attempt to find a
winning team. Here, for the sake of comparison, are the sides
selected for the various matches given in alphabetical order:

1st Test	*2nd Test*	*3rd Test*	*4th Test*	*5th Test*
Appleyard	Bailey	Bailey	Bailey	Close
Bailey	Barrington	Bedser	Compton	Compton
Barrington	Compton	Compton	Graveney	Cowdrey
Compton	Evans	Cowdrey	Insole	Ikin
Evans	Graveney	Evans	Loader	Laker
Graveney	Kenyon	Graveney	Lock	Lock
Kenyon	May	Kenyon	Lowson	May
May	Statham	Lock	May	Spooner
Statham	Titmus	May	McIntyre	Statham
Tyson	Trueman	Titmus	Statham	Tyson
Wardle	Wardle	Tyson	Wardle	Watson

The selection for the fifth match was afterwards varied in
two respects.

Twenty-five separate players. Even though injuries
accounted for some of the shake-up all this dodging in and
out of the team was not good for co-ordinated effort.

The ways of cricket Selectors are sometimes as puzzling
as the maze of Hampton Court. So I thought when I heard
with astonishment of the omission of Trevor Bailey from the
side as originally announced. Looked at in bald type his
scores in the series were not spectacular—49 in the first Test;
13 and 22 in the second; 44 and 38 not out in the third;
9 (as an opener) and 8 in the fourth. His eight wickets in the
four matches included those of McGlew, and Endean in the
first Test; Cheetham in the second; and Keith in the third.

Modest performances on paper certainly, but what a rallying point the innings of Bailey were over and over again. Even the eight runs of his second attempt in the fourth Test had been a focal point of resistance. For the hours he had spent at the wicket making his runs you must consult my reports of the various matches. And always Bailey was ready to chip in with a spell of attacking or defensive bowling when the users of the new ball needed a rest.

Apart from May and Compton, Bailey was our most consistent batsman. It was said he was dropped because he was not "positive enough", whatever that may mean. It is little use for a batsman to be "positive" if this sterling quality straightway gets him out. Time and time again Bailey "stuck it" after more spectacular batsmen had failed. He did his excellent best for England, even though I know on one or two occasions he would have preferred, for domestic reasons, to be at home at Leigh-on-Sea.

To throw out a man with this record of consistency was to my mind sheer folly. Bailey's record in the recent past was outstanding. But for him, indeed, we should not have regained the Ashes in 1953, for his match-saving stand with Willie Watson at Lord's enabled England to live and fight and win another day at the Oval. In Australia in 1954–5 his services had been equally outstanding. In nine Test Match innings there he averaged 37, and in the series he took ten wickets at 30·6.

I know it falls to the lot of every player who goes on long enough to be dropped, and Bailey had played about 30 Test Matches. But he is only 31, with years of useful cricket ahead of him.

So used had we become to regarding Bailey as an automatic choice for England because of his all-round ability that his omission aroused national discussion. The cartoonists got busy on the subject. My colleague Maroc, of the *Evening Standard*, produced a sketch showing the boss of a business talking severely to an employee. The boss said something like this:

"Even in these days of full employment no one can consider himself indispensable. See what's happened to Trevor Bailey."

Bailey, like Brer Rabbit, "lay low and say nuffin' ". No cricketer ever does say anything in such circumstances. Yet two days later he produced concrete comment in the form of 152 not out for Essex against Kent. We had dropped the anchor, cable and all, just at a time when our side needed firm anchoring more than anything else.

Fate, however, intervened to reverse this blunder. A whole crop of injuries in the week before the game drove the Selectors and captain to distraction. To take the least serious of them, Compton jammed a finger in the door of a motor-car. Just the sort of thing that *would* happen to our rather happy-go-lucky hero. The finger was blackened and sore, and three days before the Test Match began a knock he took on it from Bannister of Warwickshire did it no good, but he was able to play.

During that same game between Middlesex and Warwickshire at Lord's Laker turned up as a spectator. He had not gone down to Somerset to share in the harvest of easy wickets reaped by Lock and Bedser. The spinning fingers of his bowling hand were sore. He also was passed fit without much ado.

But there was a lot of ado about three others, Tyson, Watson and Cowdrey. Several days before the match it was known that Watson had hurt his right hand. Up he came to London for treatment by a specialist.

Tyson was the next problem. His left heel was worrying him. Over he went from Northamptonshire, where he was playing for his County, to Clacton-on-Sea for treatment by his friend the Essex masseur and physiotherapist, Harold Dalton, who knew Tyson well while both were with the M.C.C. side in Australia. The Selectors, and incidentally the newspapers, knew all about these in plenty of time. But two days before the match Cowdrey became a casualty. He hurt himself again on the same right forefinger as a ball from Heine originally hit during the third Test Match. Other bowlers had touched it up when Cowdrey was playing for Kent, and then, lo and behold, Preston's bowling put the finishing touch when the Kent side were playing Essex at Clacton-on-Sea.

The three "invalids", Tyson, Watson and Cowdrey, were invited to "do their stuff" in the nets at Lord's on the eve of the Test Match. Allen, Ames, May and various others watched the fitness test. Watson, whose hand had greatly improved, passed with first-class honours. Tyson bowled first very gently and then with something like his normal flying run. He also batted. Cowdrey batted, too, but rather gingerly, and it was pretty obvious he was not fit.

Half an hour or so after this trial by ordeal Allen announced that Watson was fit and would play, but that neither Tyson nor Cowdrey would do so. Two of the "old hands", Graveney and Bailey, from previous Tests, were restored to their places.

Bailey, quite irrespective of what would happen at the Oval, had thoroughly earned his place. About Graveney's claim to reinstatement one felt more doubtful. His Test innings in this series had been 42, 15, 60, 0, 1, 10, and 36. To say the least of it he was a fortunate man, but the ability was there and one wished him well.

Many a critic, particularly from the North, advocated the claims of Trueman, who the previous day had done the hat trick for his County. He had not bowled well in the one Test he had played, and the Selectors apparently felt that neither Trueman nor any other fast bowler available could live up to the Tysonic standard. The Selectors knew that the Oval wicket would make the fifth Test a spinner's match, and they felt that in Bailey they had a fast bowler who would do what was needed in that department and also make runs.

Here indeed, then, was a transformation. On the Monday Bailey had been ditched. On the Friday he was called up from Clacton as the very bowler and batsman England needed.

What of the opposition? Between the fourth Test Match and the fifth the South Africans went on from strength to strength. They drew at Stoke-on-Trent in their own favour a two-day fixture against the Minor Counties. Some of the Englishmen in this match had had first-class experience. Next they played at Swansea against Glamorgan which, curiously enough, is the only County favoured by the South Africans with two fixtures. The touring side won by 226 runs, and in the process dismissed Glamorgan in the first innings for 64 runs, their lowest score of the season. Heine in that innings took five for 26.

Thence they went on to Birmingham and beat Warwickshire, one of the strongest half-dozen counties, by ten wickets. In these two matches Cheetham returned to captain the side. The game against Gloucestershire at Cheltenham was left drawn. A strange and unfamiliar substance called "rain" interfered in the proceedings. At one time the County seemed to have a fair chance of victory, for they set the South Africans the task of making 214 in their second innings. The opening batsmen were out for a single apiece, but Cheetham and McLean saved the situation and the draw was rather in the South African's favour. They ended with 108 for three.

The last match for the South Africans before the fifth Test was that at Leicester, and in beating the County by an innings and 117 runs they won their ninth victory in the last twelve matches. Against the County sides they had become as unbeatable as any touring Australians.

McGlew and Keith made centuries, Tayfield and Mansell each bagged eight wickets. Adcock came back for the first time since his injury, and he took two wickets, but as he had not had enough hard practice he did not regain his place in the Test Match side. On the other hand Cheetham, who had had more recent play than Adcock, resumed the captaincy. The side, which was not announced until the morning of the match at the Oval, had two changes from the one which won at Leeds. Winslow stood down for Cheetham and Adcock for Fuller, who had bowled in the first Test Match but had been dropped for the next three.

These then were the sides, the Englishmen with five changes now that Bailey and Graveney were back, the South Africans with only two.

CHAPTER XII

THE FIFTH TEST MATCH

*Played at Kennington Oval on Saturday, 13th August,
and won by England by 92 runs on the fourth day of
the match, Wednesday, 17th August, at 5.15 p.m.*

HERE indeed was a memorable match—in many respects
the best of the five. Not until the last day was well
advanced could the winner be foreseen. Many were the feats
to entertain enormous crowds on every one of the four days.

On the English side was the batting of the young captain
Peter May, who, with inadequate support, upheld the English
second innings and made victory possible. On the English
side also was a courageous innings by Denis Compton under
the handicap of a swollen and painful knee—*the* knee!

And, as will be related in detail below, there was an outstanding bowling performance by the Surrey spinners, Tony
Lock and Jim Laker, which finally clinched our victory.

The losers also won abundant honours. Jackie McGlew
played two stubborn innings; John Waite tried desperately hard
on the last day to turn defeat into victory; and Tayfield the spinner
bowled 52 consecutive overs on the last day but one of the game.

Finally, the whole side gave a display of fielding which
picked them out not only as cricketers but as athletes. They
tumbled about like a collection of first-class soccer goal-
keepers. Indeed, I can cordially commend McGlew, Goddard
and McLean and several others to, say, the Arsenal, Aston
Villa and Newcastle United. If they can stop a small ball
with such unfailing regularity they ought to be able to deal
with any penalty kicks that are going.

Now to the details of this match which, Englishman though
I am, I was sorry in some ways to see the South Africans
lose. They had recovered so splendidly after early reverses,
and matched our technical skill and long experience with a
skill of their own and abundant enthusiasm.

FIRST DAY

England won the toss for the fourth time in five matches,
batted and scored 70 for one wicket in the two and a
half hours during which play was possible.

How great an anti-climax was this Saturday of the match
that really mattered! The previous month or more of settled
weather had deluded us into feeling that "it ain't goin' to
rain no more". But rain it did and three and a half hours of
the opening day's cricket were lost to the 25,000 spectators
who crowded into Kennington Oval.

Of the sun nothing was seen all day long, but there was
no stoppage of play during the morning. After lunch there
was one interruption of half an hour, and from 3.15 onwards
not a ball could be bowled. The prophets, who are so often
wrong, had told us that winning the toss would mean winning
the match. They were right this time. Peter May, much luckier
in that respect than his forerunner Len Hutton, spun to
Cheetham's call and won again. Only at Leeds had the
South Africans called aright.

Inevitably England batted, taking what risk there was of
before-lunch liveliness in the wicket. At the Oval only the
previous week the first four Surrey wickets had fallen to the
Middlesex bowlers for six runs; fortunately there was no
repetition of that calamity. The sky was overcast, the light
dull, and the whole outlook drab in contrast with the recent
sunny scenes in Manchester and Leeds.

All sorts of pairings had been forecast for our opening
couple. Ikin, Watson, Close, Cowdrey (until his injury),
Graveney—any two of these were tipped for the responsibility of setting the England innings going. The score-card
mentioned Ikin and Watson. But captains are not bound by
score-cards, and, following the South African fieldsmen into
the middle as they took the field, were a pair of left-handers,
Ikin of Lancashire and Close of Yorkshire.

The idea obviously was to counter the left-handed bowling
of Goddard, whose persistent attack on and near the leg-
stump had puzzled and held up our right-hand batsmen. Well

as Close had recently batted for Yorkshire in the number two position here was a risky experiment indeed. The young man's Test record had been limited to two not very successful appearances further down the batting list.

Old hands—and I fear I must count myself one—could not remember an instance of an English innings opening with two left-handers.

The first overs of a Test Match always have something of the same sort of atmosphere as "match point" in the final of the Wimbledon Singles. Everyone hopes, or fears, that something drastic will happen. In this case nothing did for quite a while. The first ball, bowled by Heine from the Vauxhall end to Ikin, produced an ineffective appeal for l.b.w. The ball in my judgment would easily have jumped over the top of the stumps. It hit Ikin in the midriff. The appeal was derided by a very lively section of onlookers clustering under the major gasometer. The over was a maiden after the approved Test Match pattern.

From the pavilion end Goddard bowled. In the past his turns have spread out to an hour or two. This time his opening spell lasted for only two overs. Whether it was the left-hand batting which made Cheetham take him off I do not know, but so he did. In the first of these two overs Close took a single off the opening ball and a no-ball allowed Ikin a nice safe two to give him a start.

The early scoring rate was, to say the least of it, no slower than is usual in Test Matches. Runs came in singles and twos, and Close drove Heine for a three. Goddard was succeeded by Fuller, who is not quite so fast as Heine but brings the ball sharply off the pitch.

The first boundary of the match came after 25 minutes—a cut by Ikin off Heine. This brought our score to 18—each man nine. By now our pair had beaten the sorry performance at Leeds where the two English innings began with partnerships of 15 and three. Close, too, cut Heine for four and gained on his partner in scoring.

Not everyone in this crowd was keyed up into a state of nervous exhaustion. Below me a woman spectator was calmly knitting, an activity having a sombre historical precedent. The upper windows of Archbishop Tenison's Grammar School, endowed long before Kennington Oval or cricket was dreamt of, were well tenanted by boys and old boys.

After an hour the total reached 39, by far the best English opening since the first Test Match at Nottingham where Kenyon and Graveney put on 91. Soon afterwards came a misfortune which changed the English innings for the worse. A ball bowled by Heine struck Ikin in the body. He doubled up in pain. The South Africans clustered round him, and after two or three minutes' attention he resumed play. But only temporarily. An over later Ikin walked slowly off the field with his own score 15, that of Close 25, and the total 43 in an hour and a quarter.

This accident brought in Peter May, who never looked like staying and indeed did not stay very long. He experienced one of those days, which all batsmen share, of inability to find touch. If Ikin's innings had not been interrupted May's early downfall might not have happened. He ran a two in leg-byes and got off the mark with a single off Heine. Later he added two more singles to his score. Then after a stay of 25 minutes, he gave Goddard a catch at second slip, straight to the fieldsman. Fifty-one for one, Close now 28 and joined by Compton.

On this morning Cheetham pinned all his faith on the fast bowlers. Heine, who is big, strong and apparently tireless, continued in charge of the Vauxhall end until ten minutes before lunch. By then he had bowled 15 overs for 34 runs. Goddard was his successor. At the other end Fuller had no rest before lunch from the time he began his bowl at 11.50.

The last over bowled by Goddard before the interval was fatal to Close. He lashed out and edged the ball high over the slips. No one could have grumbled at Mansell if he had missed a very high and difficult chance, but he jumped as the ball was passing over him and took the catch. Fifty-nine for two.

Close had very well justified the Selectors in bringing him back into Test cricket. His 32 had been made without a chance, McLean, who does not miss much, had waited expectantly on the boundary for an offering from one of Close's hook shots but it had not come.

Lunch was taken immediately Close was out with the total 59 for two, Compton four.

We in the Press box, like everyone in the crowd outside, felt concerned about Ikin. We remembered that two years before he had undergone a major operation. The doctor called to the Oval dressing-room was reassuring, the feeling of sickness passed and after lunch Ikin reappeared with Compton amid cheers.

The only addition to Ikin's score was a two he hit off Goddard. At 62, after ten minutes of afternoon play, his innings was again interrupted, this time by rain. After half an hour the players came out again, though the light was dull and every minute seemed likely to be the last. Compton made two or three nice strokes, including a four swept by him to the pavilion rails off Goddard.

Heine took over from Goddard with fatal results for Ikin. The bowler had to thank Waite for a magnificent catch behind the wicket, one worthy of Godfrey Evans himself. Waite threw himself on his side at full stretch, and held the ball, snicked by Ikin, with the back of his glove on the ground. Sixty-nine for three—Ikin 17, a typically stubborn effort worth more than the actual figures indicate.

Watson was the newcomer, but had time only to score a single before rain intervened again. This time there was no resumption. It was disheartening to see this vast crowd, which had been keyed up to enjoy the cricket, filtering out dejectedly through the gates until the arena was surrounded by nothing more animated than sodden waste paper.

Neither side had gained any great advantage from the two and a half hours' cricket. On paper, I suppose, the South Africans had reason for congratulations, but with the prospect of more rain they had reason to fear the prowess of Lock and Laker later in the match.

SECOND DAY

*England's innings was completed for 151 runs. The
South Africans were all out for 112.*

In other words 17 wickets—seven English and ten South
African—fell in the six hours of this Monday for 193 runs and
England gained a first innings lead of 39.

One glance at the ground as about 28,000 people gathered
for the second day's play was enough to indicate that trouble
lay ahead of the batsmen. The rainless Sunday had been far
from sufficient to dry the wicket. It was obviously soft—an
impression confirmed by the dark brown of the worn pitches
left by previous matches. Piles of sawdust lay at each end; the
bowlers were constantly having to attend to their footholds.
Prophets of a bowlers' day were completely vindicated.

It was a more cheerful sort of morning by far than Saturday
—bright, almost dazzling, and warm enough for the discarding
of coats by both sexes. The vast perimeter of the ground was
an expanse of summery-looking clothing.

Before Compton, 12, and Watson, 1, resumed their innings
the heavy roller was applied to squeeze the water to the surface
and make batting easier until the sun dealt with this new
moisture.

The fourth ball of the day, bowled by Heine, was only
half-stopped by Compton, but he clapped his bat down on it
in time to prevent a trickle on to his stumps. The last ball of
the over, which bounced head high, he hooked for two.

The bowler at the other end was that spry young red-head
Fuller. In his run up he tore out with his foot a divot in front
of the wicket. Umpire Bartley took a look at it and replaced
it with his foot.

Compton of late had been unable to keep his hands out
of trouble. Now, facing Heine, he took a knock on the left
hand; it was his right that recently caught itself in a car door.
The damage this time did not seem to be serious, for just
afterwards Compton used that short-arm hook of his against
Heine. Tayfield, running hard across the outfield, turned the
value of the stroke from four to two.

The fielding of the South Africans was superb. Waite behind the wicket seemed to be an extra fine leg and an extra "slipper" as well as wicketkeeper. McGlew threw himself about fearlessly to halve the value of the Englishmen's strokes. Fielding such as this serves a double purpose. Not only does it cut down the runs, but it tends to make batsmen take risks in order to elude the sentinels.

In half an hour our two batsmen were still there, but the South Africans, knowing that the wicket would become worse, might well have been pleased at having limited the runs to a dozen. Tayfield and Goddard were powerful reinforcements to bring into action at the appropriate moment.

Watson, hooking Heine for three, made the first stroke of the morning worth more than two runs. A ball from Fuller jumped from one of Compton's fingers on to his chest. McLean advanced with an enquiry about his health, and, taking the bat from Compton, patted the ground for him. *Toujours la politesse.*

On came Tayfield after 40 minutes of Heine, with the total by now raised from 70 to 83. Until he found his length the new bowler was just a little expensive; Watson drove him for a single and Compton for the first boundary of the day. But once Tayfield had settled down very little could be done with him.

At the other end Fuller, given a much longer spell than Heine had, was almost as economical as Tayfield; but once Watson hit him hard over the heads of two fieldsmen for his first boundary.

After an hour the total was exactly 100. It had not been a quick century—three and a half hours on two days. Goddard was now bowling instead of Fuller, whose eight overs had cost only 13 runs.

Compton had an adventure when 28. He pulled Goddard hard round to mid-wicket, where McLean threw out an optimistic hand, but the ball was just out of reach. This did not greatly matter, because Compton was out soon afterwards, with the total 105. Goddard had maintained his leg-stump attack against him and Compton is not the man to submit to such tactics indefinitely. Several times he tried to sweep the ball to the boundary, with indifferent success. Now he tried again fatally. He hit the ball much too "thin", as the billiards people say, and Waite, throwing himself sideways, made another splendid catch. Compton had batted two hours and a few minutes for his 30, and he and Watson had added 36 together. Now play had been in progress for an hour and twenty minutes. In point of time and productivity it was the longest English stand of the day. From then onwards wickets began to fall in a slide.

Graveney replaced Compton and Watson continued to make encouraging strokes—until he was out ten minutes after Compton's departure. Then Mansell caught him beautifully in the slips off Tayfield. He had batted an hour and a half that day and a few minutes on the Saturday for 25 runs. One hundred and seventeen for five.

Trevor Bailey, who followed in, had been criticised as being "too negative". This time he was altogether too positive. The "Barnacle"—to use his slightly impolite nickname—fell to Tayfield. Whether by accident or design, that wily bowler plied Bailey with a long hop which tempted him into making a full-out hook stroke before his eye was thoroughly in. He lifted the ball and was caught by Heine about half-way out to the boundary. This wicket, like the previous one, had fallen at 117; in other words Bailey had made a duck—his first indiscretion of the kind in this series. After all, Bailey is not an automatic machine for manufacturing runs.

Spooner's stay was hardly longer than Bailey's and no more productive. After Graveney had scored a single Spooner tried to tickle to leg a full toss from Tayfield. He missed it and it bowled him. One hundred and eighteen for seven, Graveney now four.

Hereabouts Tayfield had taken in 28 balls three wickets or one run. This, of course, is just an excerpt from his overall figures, which, though, creditable, were not as sensational as this. Laker remained with Graveney until lunch time—122 for seven, Graveney six in 40 minutes and Laker two.

Eight minutes after play was resumed Laker was out to a catch of the best South African pattern. Goddard followed up his own bowling far down wicket, fell almost flat and caught

Three "pairs" of interest in the last Test Match of
the series. England's opening batsmen, Ikin (*right*) and Close.
Laker and Lock, the two England spin bowlers whose attack shattered the South African batting. The
umpires, Messrs. D. Davies (*shorter*) and T. Bartley, taking the field

FIFTH TEST

Lock's close field, two slips, silly point, silly mid-off and short leg with
Waite batting in the final Test Match, second day at the Oval

England's captain, Peter May, acknowledging the cheers of the crowd from the balcony in the pavilion at the Oval, after his team had won the final Test and rubber

The victorious England team that beat South Africa by 92 runs at the Oval. *Back row* (*left to right*) : D. Morgan (who substituted for Compton on the last day), B. Statham, W. Watson, T. Graveney, T. Lock, B. Close and D. Spooner. *Front row* (*left to right*): J. Ikin, P. May (captain), T. Bailey and J. Laker

and bowled the batsman. One hundred and twenty-three for eight. Graveney at this late stage in the innings determined to make what runs he could while he could. He cut Tayfield for two, drove the next ball for four and tried a grand slam at each of the ensuing three, only to bang the ball to a band of fieldsmen capable of stopping anything except an express train. This flurry of runs from Graveney was brief, for he sent a hook to Fuller in the middle distance at leg. The catch, taken low down by this fine fieldsman, was as spectacular as others had been. One hundred and thirty for nine. Graveney had made 13 in 50 minutes' batting. The manner of his departure could not be criticised. If he had had a first-class batsman to stay with him he would have acted differently.

Lock and Statham were the last pair, and resolute hitting, chiefly by Lock, yielded 21 runs. Twice did Lock drive Tayfield to the boundary; a third four came in a less laudable manner from a snick off Goddard. The innings was over for 151. Goddard had five for 31, and Tayfield three for 39. The credit was equally shared, for although Goddard's figures were rather better it was the triple success of Tayfield between one o'clock and 1.15 which broke the back of the English innings.

This total was certainly no subject for letter-writing home. Yet one felt, before the South Africans received a single ball, that trouble lay ahead of them. It did not come immediately, for the heavy roller had again been applied, but come it certainly did.

Statham opened the bowling, and Bailey was restored, because of the absence of Tyson, to his old place as joint leader of our attack. After three overs from him, Lock was brought on in his place at the pavilion end. He gave the ball a rub on the turf for shine-removing purposes. Two balls in his first over, which was a maiden, beat Goddard, but it was Bailey who took the first wicket. He had not been given a rest but was moved to the Vauxhall end in Statham's place. The transfer succeeded, for Goddard was l.b.w. with the total 22.

Despite this success, Laker was soon brought into partnership with Lock, as expected, in an all-Surrey spin attack. McGlew and the new batsman Keith had to defend their wickets desperately. Laker was able to bowl apparently

I

unending maiden overs, but Lock was the greater menace to the batsmen. With the total 29 Keith, playing forward to him, was beaten and the ball hit the top of the off stump.

Endean, the new batsman, lasted only ten minutes. One was surprised indeed that he lasted so long, for he looked quite helpless against Lock. Then he gave Ikin, standing at point, a catch so simple that most grandmothers could have taken it. Thirty-one for three.

McLean was the next batsman and scored one more run than Endean. That is to say he scored a single. I would not say that McLean's supreme virtue is patience. He hates having to sit on the splice. With the total 33 he flourished his bat in a veritable "cow shot" and was bowled. Lock's figures at that point were 8·2—4—6—3. He was bowling to a hotly attacking field, with half a dozen fieldsmen clustering round the bat. Here let me mention how the "near-the-bat" fielding was strengthened by the presence of Ikin. Lock, unfortunately, could not take post close to the wicket to his own bowling; Ikin was a highly efficient substitute—except for one missed chance in the second innings.

Before and after tea little McGlew, with the resolute jutting chin of a Captain Kettle, and the taller Waite joined in the best partnership of the innings. Between four o'clock and 5.35 they scored 44 runs together, raising the total to 74. They disarranged the bowling to the extent that Lock and Laker changed ends through the intervention of a single over from Statham. Lock eventually was given a rest and Statham returned to bowl in real earnest.

This troublesome stand was ended just when danger arose that it would outlive the bad wicket. Laker had Waite out, thanks to a tumbling catch by Lock at short leg.

Seventy-seven for five became 77 for six only five minutes later when McGlew's innings was ended by a catch at the wicket as he tried to drive Statham. The South African vice-captain had shown, during two hours, tremendous powers of concentration and defence. Most certainly he had been throughout the series the most consistent batsman on either side. Look at his innings—68, 51, in the first Test, a pair of spectacles blotting his copybook in the second; 104 not out and 48 in the third; 23 and 133 in the fourth; and 30 and 19 in the fifth.

Of the remainder of the South African innings there is no need to write at length. Mansell was l.b.w. to Laker for six—86 for seven—Tayfield and Fuller departed for small scores and Cheetham, in for nearly an hour, could find no one to stay with him. The last man, Heine, joined him with the total 98, and in a final attempt to approach our total they took theirs to 112. Then that wholehearted cricketer Lock chased a drive from Cheetham, and returned the ball so quickly and so straight that Heine was run out in trying to scramble a third run.

Lock's part in the day's proceedings had indeed been prodigious. He had scored 18 runs at a time when his batting seniors had tied themselves into knots; he had taken the wickets of Keith, Endean, McLean and Fuller for 39 runs; in one period of fifteen minutes he bagged the first three of them for six runs in 50 balls. He had made a very good catch and been the chief actor in a run-out.

I had had letters criticising my preference for Lock as against Wardle for this match on Lock's own ground—but really! Wardle must be a super-cricketer to beat this all-round display.

For England it had been a good day, but it might have been even better if our batsmen had chanced their arm more in the morning while the pitch was soggy. The idea ought to have been to make quick runs while the wicket was relatively innocuous and then set the opposition to bat directly it became bad. Instead of which the morning two hours yielded only 52 runs.

THIRD DAY

*England in their second innings scored 195 for eight,
and at the end of the day held a lead of 234.*

Nobody watching this third day's play, during which the Englishmen tried to build a winning lead, could call it snappy entertainment. One hundred and ninety-five runs in a six-hour day is only a little over one run every two minutes, and there were periods when the rate of progress was far slower than this. I propose to go into the reasons for this crawl a little later; for the time being let me stress how dull it seemed. Here was no triumphant gallop; rather did it seem a lagging march towards a goal still a wearisome way ahead.

The crowd the day before had numbered 28,500; that day's assembly looked much the same, and again three men out of every four sat coatless in the hot sunshine. How all those packed thousands "stuck it" day after day I cannot imagine. That they did so shows their deep love of cricket.

Again the two left-handers, Close and Ikin, opened the England innings. This time their partnership was like five others by English openers in previous Tests: it was not worth double figures. Close took a three off Heine and a two off Fuller, who in checking the pace of this return hurt his left hand. It seemed, from the rough and ready first aid going on out there, that a finger was dislocated. Apparently the trouble was set to rights, and Fuller continued bowling. Fortunately he is a right-hander.

Soon afterwards Ikin was out for a duck, with those five runs by Close the only score. Ikin fenced at a ball from Heine and touched it into the slips, where those good neighbours, Mansell and Goddard, brought off a joint catch. Mansell, seeing he could not accomplish it himself, nudged the ball on to Goddard, who secured it.

Here May varied his batting order, sending in Graveney instead of going in himself. The assumption was that he wanted Compton to bat lower down in the order and so promoted Graveney. Compton's gammy right knee was giving him trouble again; he had hurt it in chasing a ball the previous day, and had been under treatment evening and morning. When he arrived at the ground the leg was strapped up from thigh to ankle.

Graveney's promotion did his batting good. He played, as I thought, the best innings of the day, though not the largest. In the first half hour the loss of Ikin caused the scoring to slacken and only 15 were on the board. Once Close almost ran himself out by backing up too enthusiastically; but he scrambled home just in time to beat the throw-in. All through the six hours of this hot and trying day the South African fielding was superb. There was only one mistake of any consequence, and no runner could take the slightest risk.

In an hour the total was 26. Goddard bowled instead of Heine, and Close took the first boundary of the day with a cut off the new bowler. The change was a double one, for Tayfield relieved Fuller. He went on—and on—and on—with his bowling until the shades of night were falling fast. Later in the day the wicket became easy, but in the early hours it was still green and the ball from the fast bowlers slipped through pretty quickly.

The mid-morning drinks were taken, and then, with the total 30, Close was bowled by Goddard after batting for an hour and ten minutes for 15. One sympathised with him, for the ball merely flicked the off-side bail before passing on into the wicketkeeper's gloves.

Now May came in at number four, which is Compton's usual place. He was destined to bat all day and still remain unconquered. He and Graveney laid the foundations of our sizable total by scoring 65 runs together. The first ball received by May hit him on the pads and Goddard appealed for l.b.w. amid derision from the ringside. Later that same over he broke his duck with a drive for three.

Graveney, not to be outdone, contributed the most spectacular blow yet—one of his full-out boundary hits, an off-drive from Tayfield struck with free swing of the bat. One hardly knew whether to admire this stroke more or less than the gymnastics by which, just afterwards, Goddard prevented Graveney from repeating his feat. He threw his long length at the ball and turned four runs into one.

May, for a while, was not very happy when Tayfield bowled to him. There was one appeal, louder and more confident than usual, for l.b.w. Umpire Bartley of Cheshire decided in the batsman's favour, and May as an act of thankfulness cover-drove the next ball to the boundary.

When the innings was an hour and a half old Graveney brought up the 50 with another of his drives past Goddard, then bowling. Behind him fielded Tayfield, who threw himself flat in a vain attempt to prevent the ball from rattling the

pavilion rails. Ten minutes before lunch Mansell, whose value
to the side lay chiefly in his slip fielding, became the fifth
bowler of the morning with his leg-spinners. At 61 for two, the
total at the interval, honours were just about easy. Graveney
had batted an hour and 50 minutes for 30, and May 50
minutes for 15.

Immediately after lunch Goddard did some more athletic
fielding which drew the crowd's applause. It saved a certain
four by the England captain, who seemed to regard the
action as a challenge. Presently, throwing all he knew into
the stroke, May tried again, and this time even Goddard
could only stand and watch.

Now came the fastest scoring of the day. While Tayfield
pegged away untiringly with only a rare run against him,
Mansell provided the batsmen with 22 in four overs. The
score advanced by 24 in 20 minutes. It was too good to last.
Mansell was taken off in favour of Heine.

There seemed no reason why this May-Graveney partnership should not in fullness of time reach the century. Actually
it fell 38 runs short of it. Graveney was bowled by Tayfield
in trying to drive him. Graveney had batted about two and a
half hours for his 42. Slow going, but the innings had its
moments. It was rather like a cake with rich and luscious
plums rather too rarely distributed.

This wicket was the hundredth taken by Tayfield in Test
cricket against various countries. No other South African has
accomplished the feat.

Compton now came in. A lurch in his walk showed that
the knee was troubling him, and as time went on he became
more and more laboured in his running. His first four runs
arose from a snick off Heine, who appealed in vain for l.b.w.
Everything seemed to combine to overstrain Compton's leg.
Soon he had to go full tilt for four runs for a cut by May
which stopped just short of the boundary. That, in itself,
could have done the knee no good, and there were various
sharp singles easy for May but difficult for the other fellow.
Necessarily Compton was handicapped in his batting as well
as his running. But now and then he got in a sturdy blow.
His ability to hook was unimpaired. Compton had made ten,

and the total was 114, when something happened to show that these South African fieldsmen are human beings, suffering from human frailty. Keith, fielding in the slips to Heine, missed Compton, and missed him badly.

At tea, after a wearisome slow period, the total was 121 for three, May 47 and Compton 13. They had taken an hour and a quarter to add 26. In the two hours and five minutes between lunch and tea the Englishmen had scored only 60 runs.

May's approach to his half-century was slow indeed, but he reached it 20 minutes after tea. Soon afterwards came the 50 stand. But after 15 more runs Compton was out. Again Waite caught him behind the wicket on the leg side, but there was this difference. In his first innings Compton gave the catch when trying to sweep Goddard; in the second when trying to glide Fuller. One hundred and fifty-seven for four, Compton having scored 30 runs distinguished much more for courage in adversity than for his normal sparkle. He had batted for two and a quarter trying hours. So troubled did he look that one felt glad, for his sake, that he was out. How will Compton stand up to five-day Tests against the Australians next summer? If he cannot do so then it may be that on this August day of 1955 he slipped unobtrusively out of Test cricket. I devoutly hope not, for no one more than myself wants to see Compton make centuries against Australia next summer.

Tayfield, mark you, was still wheeling them down from the Vauxhall end. He had been doing so ever since about 12.30; and there he still was, in unfaltering action, right to the day's end. Watson was bowled by Fuller after only a brief stay—165 for five—and then Tayfield really came into his own. In his 46th consecutive over he had the unfortunate Trevor Bailey l.b.w. for a single—166 for six. After all the fuss about Bailey's original omission from the side he had scored nought and one. Do not let this doleful fact diminish admiration for Bailey as a cricketer. There never was a batsman—not even W.G. or Jack Hobbs or Don Bradman or Len Hutton—who did not crash like this on occasion. In Bailey's case the unfortunate thing is that the crash came at the wrong moment.

Tayfield followed up his success by completing Spooner's pair of spectacles for him, but Laker stayed with May to some purpose until he also was bowled by Tayfield.

At the close Lock, who had not yet scored, was with May, then 81 not out. May had been batting ever since 12.40—four hours and 50 minutes. Why was he, and the others, so slow? The answer surely must be that responsibility for displays of this sort rest with the rulers of the game who impose five-day Test Matches on us. Think how much more enterprising the Englishmen's tactics must have been with only one day more for winning the match! Risks would certainly have been taken and the whole entertainment made brighter.

The duty of a Test captain like May and his men is to win the match. If victory is more likely to arise from slow batting than from moving briskly then slow batting is justifiable. If men are set to play five-day Test Matches then they cannot be blamed for playing five-day cricket.

May would have been blamed, and rightly blamed, if in face of this very efficient South African bowling he and his side had got themselves out cheaply and left the adversaries a chance to win at their leisure.

Surely if a cricket match cannot be finished in four days it is not worth playing. Far better an occasional draw than this long-drawn-out campaign of attrition into which Test cricket has degenerated.

FOURTH DAY

England were all out for 204 which, adding in the first innings advantage of 39, meant that South Africa must make 244 to win. They were all out for 151, and England won the match by 92 and with it the rubber.

A day of fluctuating fortunes was this, right to the very end. From an English point of view it had a disappointing beginning, for the two English tail-enders, Lock and Statham, could not stay with their captain. In twelve minutes the innings was over and May had no chance of completing his century.

The crowd, for some strange reason, was smaller than on the Monday and Tuesday, even though the climax of the game lay ahead.

Heine reopened the bowling to Lock, who had not scored overnight, with the total 195 for eight. A single to Lock and another to May came in the first over, but the fourth ball had Lock l.b.w.—the first of a long series of such decisions throughout the day.

In came Statham, the last man, and survived, rather precariously, the last two balls bowled by his opposite number on the visiting side. On the old principle of setting a thief to catch a thief one would imagine that a fast bowler or a spin bowler, bat in hand, would be well equipped to frustrate the arts and wiles he employs so well himself; it does not work out that way.

Now May, obviously, had to "farm the bowling". He took a single off the last ball of the ensuing over from Tayfield, and so faced Heine again. Another single came off the fifth ball of the fast bowler's second over. But when Tayfield's turn came back the end arrived. May made the only forceful stroke of the partnership, a straight drive for four, followed by a single. This brought Statham opposite Tayfield, and he in turn was l.b.w.

May had been the mainstay of England's batting for five hours and had hit ten fours in his 89. Apart from him, Graveney and Compton, who was a cripple, May had had scant support.

Hugh Tayfield finished triumphantly his marathon bowling effort, which began after the first hour the previous day and ended only with the end of our innings. He bowled 53·4 overs for 29 maidens, 60 runs and five wickets. There surely can be no better bowler of his type in the world. Not only does he take wickets, but he keeps down the runs. Notice that in this long spell he cost his side only a fraction more than one run per over.

When the South African innings began Compton's injured knee kept him out of the field. The twelfth man, Morgan of Derbyshire, fielded in his place.

From 11.55, when McGlew faced the first over from Statham, until 12.50 the opening batsmen, McGlew and Goddard, gave us quite an anxious time. They did not score quickly—indeed 28 was their total crop of runs together—but they appeared to be digging in very nicely. Eight runs came during the first two overs—a snick by McGlew for four between first and second slip off Statham and two two's round to square leg by Goddard off Bailey. Twice Lock emulated the South Africans in smart and eager fielding near the bat.

The two fast bowlers could make small impression on the indomitable little right-hander McGlew and the tall stolid left-hander Goddard. Goddard did make one mistake. He gave a chance off Bailey to Close at first slip a couple of feet from the ground when 13. It was not accepted.

Laker was brought on for Statham at the Vauxhall end as the first bowling change. Goddard did not seem to like him a little bit. Bailey was retained for a couple of overs longer before Lock joined in an all-Surrey attack. Bailey had bowled six overs for 15 runs and a missed catch.

The scoring slowed down to almost nothing, so ultra-careful were the batsmen in face of the spinners. Then, at 28 in the score-book and 12.50 of the clock, there began an avalanche of wickets. First Goddard edged a ball from Lock neatly to Graveney at first slip. This chance was accepted. With the score unaltered Keith was out to the fourth ball he received, sending a catch to May at silly mid-on. Twenty-eight for one had become 28 for two, and Keith was the first of three makers of ducks.

Next over bowled by Laker, Endean was out too in trying a rash sweep at the ball, which he missed. Hence an l.b.w. decision. Twenty-nine for three. In came McLean and there were actually four runs scored, all by McGlew, before the next wicket fell. Like Endean, McLean tried an extraordinarily venturesome stroke so early in his innings at a time of crisis. He was given l.b.w. to Laker in another vain effort to sweep him. Thirty-three for four, which by a coincidence was the same position exactly as in the first innings. The same two men, McGlew and Waite, were faced with the task of mending the damage.

This 18-ball collapse is worth reproducing in score-book form. Here it is, from the second ball of the over from Lock which began the trouble:

```
Lock    –    –    w    .    .    .    w
Laker   –    –    .    .    1    .    w    .
Lock    –    –    .    2    .    .    2    .
Laker   –    –    w
```

So in 18 balls four wickets had gone for five runs.

After this, until lunch time, the cricket regained some semblance to sanity. Waite apparently believed, and not without reason, that some judicious hitting might drive the bowlers off their length. He drove a half volley from Laker for four, the first of several boundary strokes in which the cover-drive predominated. By lunch time he had overtaken and passed his partner. There were then 57 runs for four wickets, McGlew 17, Waite 20.

Some of the South African batsmen had had sorry experiences. Keith in the two innings had made five and nothing; Endean had bagged a pair; and McLean had got one and nothing—six runs between the three of them in half a dozen innings.

Ten minutes after lunch the Englishmen took the wicket they wanted more than any other. McGlew was l.b.w. to Lock in attempting a defensive stroke. Fifty-nine for five. McGlew had batted for an hour and three-quarters for 19 with characteristic stubbornness.

Waite, now joined by Cheetham, remained the chief danger to England. He was not at all overawed by the fate of his comrades, and he chose his opportunities for hitting with greater discretion. Cheetham, when six, might have been caught by May at short slip, though it was a very difficult chance. It did not greatly matter, for with the total 88 Cheetham was out to another l.b.w. decision, this time in favour of Laker. He had made 9 towards a partnership of 29 with Waite.

Two Englishmen and four South Africans went out to l.b.w. decisions that day.

Mansell, whose contributions with the bat during this series had been very modest indeed, now distinguished himself by staying with Waite for an hour and a quarter during which the total was lifted from 88 to 118. For most of this time the scoring was terribly slow; indeed the board stuck at 94 for more than ten minutes. But though the batsmen took their time they were not easy to displace. May, switching from spin to speed, brought on Statham for Lock at the pavilion end at 97.

The change ought to have succeeded for Ikin, usually a safe fieldsman close to the bat, dropped Mansell at third slip off his fellow Lancastrian's bowling. Presently the same stroke—a four hit by Waite off Laker—brought the total to 100 and Waite's own contribution to 50.

Laker continued until he had bowled 28 overs for 41 runs, and his three wickets. Then he in turn was rested and Lock bowled for the first time that day from the Vauxhall end. This broke the stand at last. Mansell tried to drive Lock and Watson made a safe catch at extra cover. One hundred and eighteen for seven.

Waite was now 60 not out and his innings was over for that figure. Laker's rest was a short one and, returning instead of Statham, he bowled Waite with the total still 118.

Tea arrived with Tayfield and Fuller together, the total now 119 and an English victory imminent. There was time before it came for another catch to be missed. Fuller was dropped by May before he had scored. He proceeded to hit a hazardous but plucky 16, including three boundaries. Then, as neither bowler could cope with him, he obliged by getting himself run out. One hundred and forty-four for nine. Tayfield and Heine delayed the end for a few minutes before Heine lifted the catch which ended the innings for 151. The catch, probably from the highest skier in the match, was well taken by Graveney.

Before the players left the field the turf was black and white with spectators willing and eager to applaud anyone in flannels who hove in sight on the pavilion balcony. They waited patiently for speeches from the captains, and eventually these speeches were delivered. I have heard in my time some dozens of them, and they do not vary very much in their complimentary references to friend and foe. These particular orations could hardly be heard in the Press box for the cheerful hubbub among the crowd.

The scores are as follows:

ENGLAND

First Innings

J. T. Ikin c Waite b Heine	17
D. B. Close c Mansell b Goddard	32
P. B. H. May c Goddard b Fuller	3
D. C. S. Compton c Waite b Goddard	30
W. Watson c Mansell b Tayfield	25
T. W. Graveney c Fuller b Goddard	13
T. E. Bailey c Heine b Tayfield	0
R. J. Spooner b Tayfield	0
J. C. Laker c and b Goddard	2
G. A. R. Lock c McLean b Goddard	18
J. B. Statham not out	4
Extras	7
Total	151

Fall of Wickets

1—51; 2—59; 3—69; 4—105; 5—117; 6—117; 7—118; 8—123; 9—130.

Bowling

	O.	M.	R.	W.
Heine	21	3	43	1
Goddard	22·4	9	31	5
Fuller	27	11	31	1
Tayfield	19	7	39	3

SOUTH AFRICA

First Innings

D. J. McGlew c Spooner b Statham	30
T. L. Goddard lbw b Bailey	8
H. J. Keith b Lock	5
W. R. Endean c Ikin b Lock	0
R. A. McLean b Lock	1
J. H. Waite c Lock b Laker	28
J. E. Cheetham not out	12
P. N. Mansell lbw b Laker	6
H. J. Tayfield b Statham	4
E. R. Fuller c Spooner b Lock	5
P. Heine run out	5
Extras	8
Total	112

Fall of Wickets

1—22; 2—29; 3—31; 4—33; 5—77; 6—77; 7—86; 8—91; 9—98.

Bowling

	O.	M.	R.	W.
Statham	15	3	31	2
Bailey	5	1	6	1
Lock	22	11	39	4
Laker	23	13	28	2

ENGLAND

SECOND INNINGS

D. B. Close b Goddard	15
J. T. Ikin c Goddard b Heine	0
T. W. Graveney b Tayfield	42
P. B. H. May not out	89
D. C. S. Compton c Waite b Fuller	30
W. Watson b Fuller	3
T. E. Bailey lbw b Tayfield	1
R. J. Spooner b Tayfield	0
J. C. Laker b Tayfield	12
G. A. R. Lock lbw b Heine	1
J. B. Statham lbw b Tayfield	0
Extras	11
Total	204

FALL OF WICKETS

1—5; 2—30; 3—95; 4—157; 5—165; 6—166; 7—170;
8—188; 9—197.

BOWLING

	O.	M.	R.	W.
Heine	25	6	44	2
Fuller	20	3	36	2
Goddard	19	10	29	1
Tayfield	53·4	29	60	5
Mansell	6	0	24	0

SOUTH AFRICA

Second Innings

D. J. McGlew lbw b Lock	19
T. L. Goddard c Graveney b Lock	20
H. J. Keith c May b Lock	0
W. R. Endean lbw b Laker	0
R. A. McLean lbw b Laker	0
J. H. B. Waite b Laker	60
J. E. Cheetham lbw b Laker	9
P. N. F. Mansell c Watson b Lock	9
H. J. Tayfield not out	10
E. R. H. Fuller run out	16
P. S. Heine c Graveney b Laker	7
Extras	1
Total	151

Fall of Wickets

1—28; 2—28; 3—29; 4—33; 5—59; 6—88; 7—118; 8—118; 9—144.

Bowling

	O.	M.	R.	W.
Statham	11	4	17	0
Bailey	6	1	15	0
Laker	37·4	18	56	5
Lock	33	14	62	4

England won by 92 runs.

CHAPTER XIII

SOMETHING ABOUT EVERYONE

EARLIER in this book I named the 16 South African players alphabetically, except for their captain and vice-captain who were given pride of place. Following the same plan now the rubber has been fought and narrowly lost let us see how they fared during a whole summer's cricket.

J. E. CHEETHAM. For him as captain this tour has been in one sense a disappointment; in another the reverse in that victory was so nearly won. It was ironical that after his injury during the second Test Match the third and fourth, the only two in which the South Africans triumphed, should have been won when someone else was in command. That someone else, of course, was his capable vice-captain Jackie McGlew.

Cheetham is not the man to harbour jealous feelings; so long as success came he would care very little who achieved it. Anyway, although his arm was in a sling for three or four weeks his brain was not so handicapped. I have no doubt that all the way through he shared fully in the South African councils of war and so had his part in the triumphs of Manchester and Leeds.

Cheetham's batting record up to the end of the Test series was moderately good. His highest score against England was his 54 in the first Test at Nottingham. Up to the end of the series with which my record ends his biggest innings against the counties was 87 not out against Somerset. Yet as a middle-of-the-order batsman he had a large number of useful performances which steadied the innings of his side. It is the timely twenties, thirties and forties from batsmen half way down the table that help to build up sizeable scores.

As a leader Cheetham was liked and followed by his men, always ready to comply with his strictest requirements about practice. As a fieldsman Cheetham set an example.

In addition to his achievements on the field he showed quite a pretty wit on the many occasions when speeches were required of him.

Test averages :

Three matches, six innings, twice not out, 96 runs, highest score 54, average 24.

D. J. McGLEW. In 1951, when McGlew, then only 22, came to England for the first time, he was played in only two Test Matches, and totalled 50 runs, of which 40 were made in one of his four innings. His modest average was 12.50. See the difference four years have made in his batting. This time his 476 runs in Test Matches were roughly 200 more than the next best of his side.

His efforts were consistency itself, apart from two ducks —and even they had a certain consistency about them—in the Test Match at Lords. He had two centuries against the full strength of England—104 not out at Manchester, when he and Goddard set the side well on the way towards a total of 521 for eight, and 133 in the fourth Test. Here the partnership of 176 between him and Goddard was the biggest of their series.

Many jests were made about the second half of his surname. I will not repeat them, but there were occasions when his batting lost in colourful attractiveness what it gained in drab dependability.

As a cover-point McGlew was always willing to fling himself about on the hardest ground in order to prevent Peter May from hitting a four. As a captain in two of the Test Matches he has reason to look back on his leadership with pride. In Australia in 1952–3 he was half way down his side's order of merit; now in England he rose to the very top.

Test averages :

Five matches, ten innings, once not out, 476 runs, highest score 133, average 52·88—by far the top of his country's list, though on the English side both May and Compton showed better figures.

N. A. T. ADCOCK. The fastest bowler South Africa possesses. Did not strike form or fitness without difficulty, for the cold and rain of the early summer were bad for a young fast bowler experiencing them for the first time. All the same, he was a choice for the first four Test Matches; in the last of these he broke a bone in his foot and so lost his place in the fifth.

His best bowling performance came in the Manchester match, where in the first innings he took the wickets of Graveney, Compton and Bailey for 52 runs, and in the second those of Graveney again, Titmus and Lock for 48. In both those innings, and in others, he had his share in the quick break-up of England's opening partnerships.

Adcock is no great shakes as a batsman, though he twice achieved an innings of six in the Tests. His second six, hit when his broken bone was in plaster, was his best display against England with the bat. On the whole he can be well satisfied with his first tour in England.

Test averages :

> *Batting—four matches, six innings, three times not out, 13 runs, highest score 6, average 4·33.*

> *Bowling—overs 126; maidens 37; runs 252; wickets 10; average 25·20.*

C. A. R. DUCKWORTH. Duckworth, the reserve wicket-keeper and youngest member of the side, probably realised before coming to England that his appearance in Test cricket depended on some accident or illness to his principal. No such misfortune happened to Waite and Duckworth had to be content with gaining experience against the counties. When he did have the gloves on he showed himself a capable deputy.

A burst of batting form in which he scored 158 and 30 not out against Northants led to his nomination in the short list for Test appearance, but it progressed no further than that.

W. R. ENDEAN. Endean on this tour did not live up to the tremendous reputation he made for himself in Australia in 1952–3 when he topped the batting averages at 48·66. One must assume that Australia's wickets suited him better than ours.

He really did come into his own in the Leeds Test Match, where his 116 not out as a middle batsman changed the South African innings from a moderate one into a total of 500. That was his only score of more than 50 in the series. In the last match of all he was unfortunate enough to bag "a pair". His performances against the counties were better.

Test averages :

> *Five matches, ten innings, once not out, 246 runs, highest score 116 not out, average 27·33.*

E. R. H. FULLER. Played only in the first and last Tests, though in my judgment this lively fast-medium bowler and sprightly fieldsman deserved something better. The best performance I saw from him all the tour was his seven for 61 in the second innings of Sussex, which won for the South Africans an unexpectedly easy victory.

In the absence of Adcock he opened the bowling in our second innings in the last Test, took the wickets of Compton and Watson, and made our batsmen's progress towards victory very difficult.

Test averages :

> *Batting—two matches, four innings, no not-out innings, 42 runs, highest score 16, average 10·50.*
>
> *Bowling—76 overs, 19 maidens, 126 runs, 6 wickets, average 21·00.*

These figures place him at the top of the bowling averages, though he cannot fairly be compared with others who bowled in every Test Match.

T. L. GODDARD. Proved himself the greatest all-round cricketer in the side. Had the distinction, shared by very few cricketers, of whom Trevor Bailey is one, of opening on occasions his country's batting and bowling. He ended the tour second only to H. J. Tayfield as a taker of Test wickets and was mid-way down the Test batting averages.

All this happened on his first overseas tour, for he came to England unproven in international cricket. I do not particularly like his style of bowling, the persistent attack on and just outside the leg stump; it slows down the game. But he was undeniably successful in this Test series.

In the one English innings of the first Test he took two wickets; in the two innings of the second seven; in the two of the third three; in the two of the fourth seven; and in the two of the fifth six.

His top scores in Test Matches was his 62 at Manchester, part of the long partnership with McGlew, and his 74 at Leeds, his share of 176 by himself and McGlew.

As a fieldsman he was fearless and agile everywhere, one of the outstanding figures whom crowds like to see in action.

Test averages:

Batting—five matches, ten innings, no not-out innings, 235 runs, highest score 74, average 23·50.

Bowling—315·4 overs, 148 maidens, 528 runs, 25 wickets, average 21·12.

He was second in the bowling averages to Fuller, who bowled only in two Tests.

P. S. HEINE. This giant in a side of giants did not come into the Test side for the first match, but displaced Fuller for the second, in which he was an immediate success, taking the wickets of Graveney, May, Compton, Barrington and Evans for 60 runs. Thereafter he was never in any danger of losing his place. His bowling, second only in pace to Adcock's, fizzed off the pitch and swung enough to beat the bat. He had good performances in every Test Match in which he played. His fielding in any position was creditable.

Test averages:

Batting—four matches, seven innings, once not out, 74 runs, highest score 22 not out, average 12·33.

Bowling—199·5 overs, 46 maidens, 494 runs, 21 wickets, average 23·52.

H. J. KEITH. Played in last four Test Matches, though his record as a left-hand bat in the number three position was uneven, and he was only once called on for a brief spell of slow bowling. His biggest Test innings was 73 in the Leeds match—the innings when half a dozen batsmen were helping themselves to runs.

Test averages:

> *Batting—four matches, eight innings, no not-out innings, 178 runs, highest score 73, average 22·25.*
>
> *Bowling—6 overs, 1 maiden, 19 runs, no wickets.*

P. N. F. MANSELL. Came to England for the second time with a reputation as a leg-spin bowler, but he played in four of the Test Matches chiefly as a batsman and slip fielder. His top score in the Tests was 16 at Lord's, and in the last innings at the Oval he delayed defeat in a long seventh-wicket partnership with Waite.

His catching of Close in the English first innings was one of the finest such efforts in the tour. If playing a man chiefly for his fielding is ever justified, then it was so in the case of Mansell. He took eight catches in the Test series.

Test averages:

> *Batting—four matches, eight innings, no not-out innings, 45 runs, highest score 16, average 5·62.*
>
> *Bowling—48 overs, 7 maidens, 130 runs, 1 wicket, average 130·00.*

His one wicket ended the innings of May at Manchester for 117.

R. A. McLEAN. We expected from McLean great things in batsmanship on his second visit to England, and at times we had them, but he was far from dependable. After a series of low scores early in the tour he played a brilliant 85 against M.C.C. and a century against Essex.

In Test Matches he played only two innings of 50 or over —142 in the second Test and 50 in the third at a time when the South Africans needed runs in a hurry. His innings in the last Test Match—one and none—were an anticlimax. McLean has not yet lost the impetuousness which sometimes defeats him. The fatal "sweep" in his second innings at the Oval, soon after he appeared in a crisis, was the species of stroke he will learn to discard.

He is rather like Neil Harvey of Australia in his propensity for giving the bowlers a chance. Sometimes he allows them far too much chance. At the same time McLean, by his batting, gave us many of the happiest hours of the tour. As an out-fielder he was fast, keen, and entirely reliable in his ground work and catching.

Test averages:
> *Five matches, ten innings, no not-out innings, 277 runs, highest score 142, average 27·70.*

A. R. A. MURRAY. An all-rounder who did not play in a Test Match, though he might have found a place but for a broken finger in mid-season. Indeed, up to the end of the fifth Test he played in only ten matches. His highest score till then was 51 against Gloucestershire and his best bowl-ing, three for 22 and one for two, was against the same County.

V. I. SMITH. Looked to me a pretty good leg-spin bowler, but he was played in only one of the five Test Matches. His record against the counties was good.

Leg-spin men have gone out of fashion these days in international cricket, and batsmen in some cases have almost forgotten how to play them. For that reason it might have been well to retain Smith in the side. Variety pays.

Test averages:
> *Batting—one match, two innings, once not out, 2 runs, highest score 2 not out, average 2.*
>
> *Bowling—30 overs, 9 maidens, 62 runs, 1 wicket, average 62·00.*

H. J. TAYFIELD. One of the greatest, perhaps the greatest, off-spin bowlers in the world. He was first seen in England four years ago when he came as an emergency reinforcement. In Australia in 1952–3 he took far more wickets than anyone else, and in England in the recent tour he was at the top of the list with 26 in Tests, though his average was fractionally less than Goddard's.

Never did he rise to greater heights than in his prolonged

effort at the Oval to pull the fifth Test Match out of the fire. Coming on at about 12.30 he bowled without rest, except for meal intervals, for the remainder of the day—52 overs costing only a little over a run each, with four wickets. His duel on that occasion with Peter May was a fascinating one. May did not fall to him, or any other bowler, in this innings, but at times Tayfield pressed him very hard.

In figures his best Test Match was the Leeds one. Here he took four for 70 and five for 94. Even when he was not taking wickets Tayfield was always dropping the ball right on the spot and was terribly difficult to punish except at extreme risk. He proved himself a useful batsman down the list and never let his side down in the field.

Test Averages:

    Batting—five matches, ten innings, three times not out, 117 runs, highest score 28, average 16·71.

    Bowling—313·3 overs, 124 maidens, 568 runs, 26 wickets, average 21·84.

In the match at the Oval Tayfield completed his hundredth wicket against Test-playing nations. A fine slip fieldsman.

J. H. B. WAITE. With McGlew, McLean, Goddard, Tayfield and Heine, was one of the great successes of the tour. As a wicketkeeper he was almost in the Evans class; sometimes one is tempted to omit the "almost". He took 14 catches in the five Tests, five of them in the Manchester match. One Test century, 113 at Manchester, and a very valiant 60, made in the hope of turning the tables at the Oval.

Test Averages:

    Second in the list to McGlew, five matches, ten innings, once not out, 265 runs, highest score 113, average 29·44.

P. L. WINSLOW. When Winslow's cricket is nearly forgotten one event will be remembered—the six hit with which he completed his century in the Test Match at Manchester. I should like to have measured it, but had no opportunity. It carried the ball over a stand into the car park. Not everyone has the nerve to clinch his one and only Test century against England in this manner.

Apart from that glorious innings, Winslow's Test record was quite modest. He played in only three of the five matches, his other scores being 2, 3, 16, 8, and 19. But Winslow plays a type of cricket giving him no very long expectation of life.

Apart from the Test Matches the feat which brought him into the newspaper headlines was his rough treatment of Ikin and Goodwin in the Lancashire match. He hit them for 40 in eight balls. Nearly always Winslow took post in the outfield. Despite those spectacles of his the loftiest skier almost invariably came to hand.

Test averages:

> *Three matches, six innings, no not-out innings, 156 runs, highest score 108, average 26.00.*

Now for the 25 Englishmen needed for five Test Matches.

PETER MAY, the captain, emulated Len Hutton in the West Indies tour in not only leading the side but heading the batting averages. Like Hutton, too, he captained England without captaining his own County, though I suspect that he owes quite a lot in the way of hints from the Surrey skipper Stuart Surridge.

In every one of the five Test Matches he played at least one innings of distinction, and, by contrast with his batting in Australia, he became more consistent. There were indeed only two innings of under 30 in the nine he played—his duck in the first innings of the second Test Match at Lord's, and his three in the fifth Test at the Oval.

His Test centuries were two; in all probability they would have been three if the tail-enders had stayed in at the Oval long enough for him to score eleven more runs; and there were two other innings very nearly as good as centuries—his 83 at Nottingham and his 97 at Leeds.

The two occasions when three-figure scores flowed from his bat were his 112 at Lord's, richly compensating for that duck, and 117 at Manchester. His stand of 124 runs with Denis Compton in the second innings at Manchester was about the finest display of batting at both ends of the pitch seen in the whole Test series. May was irreproachably correct, Compton his old unorthodox daring self.

May now seems established as the England captain for some years to come. Now that he is in the saddle it is difficult to believe that Hutton, even if he returns, will be invited to resume the captaincy. It would be bad for his batting if he were.

May, with his cheerful, happy disposition, does not seem to feel at all deeply the strain of doing the two jobs. He is younger than Hutton.

May seemed to manage his bowling with judgment and is personally well liked by his men—even when they come from Surrey's rival county Yorkshire. If there is any criticism of his leadership it lies in his reluctance to employ his occasional bowlers when his bowlers-in-chief are held up during a long stand. An over or two from Denis Compton or Tom Graveney might have the effect of separating two stubborn opponents. Batsmen are apt to take liberties against supposedly inferior bowling.

Given health and strength there is a golden cricket future for this likeable young captain, who in time will no doubt succeed to the leadership of Surrey. He is to be envied in having before him the prospect of ten or more years of top-class cricket.

Test averages:

> *Five matches, nine innings, once not out, 582 runs, highest score 117, average 72·75—easily first.*

Let us take the others in alphabetical order.

R. APPLEYARD (YORKSHIRE). Misfortune seems to dog this fine cricketer, probably the best bowler of his type in the country. He had a serious illness some years ago which kept him out of cricket for a whole season. Then, in Australia last winter, he established himself as a mainstay in our bowling. But last home season he was able to play only in the first Test Match.

An injured shoulder, which gave great trouble, kept him out of consideration for the later matches. On the one occasion he did play, at Nottingham, he took two wickets in a match in which chief honours went to Frank Tyson.

Test averages:

    Batting : one match, one innings, nought not out.

    Bowling: 47 overs, 13 maidens, 78 runs, two wickets, average 39·00.

T. E. BAILEY (Essex). In the public mind Trevor Bailey is as immovable a member of the England side as the captain himself. This notion was shattered when he was left out of the original selection for the last Test. It was rather an anticlimax that, after he had been restored to the side, his part in the match consisted of a duck and one and the capture of one wicket.

This unfortunate happening need not destroy popular faith in Bailey as a tremendous stand-by in troublous times. He proved his ability in every one of the Test Matches save the last. Even the eight runs which he scored in his second innings at Leeds came slowly during a long-drawn-out struggle against inevitable defeat.

In one innings at Leeds he was tried as an opener, but the move did not succeed.

As a bowler he was denied the first new ball until he came into the Oval Test as a deputy to the injured Tyson. That was hardly a fair trial, because the Oval wicket was a spinner's rather than a fast bowler's. As a follow-up bowler to Statham and Tyson he was invaluable in match after match—nearly always able to keep the runs down and sometimes able to take the odd wicket. He ought to be remembered with thankfulness for defeating McGlew at Nottingham when that hero had scored 51 and was seriously holding up our move towards victory.

Bailey, like most of the English team, cannot claim that he did not miss a catch in the series, but he was more reliable than the average Englishman in his fielding.

Test averages:

    Batting : Five matches, nine innings, once not out, 184 runs, highest score 49, average 23·00.

    Bowling: 142·5 overs, 40 maidens, 328 runs, 9 wickets, average 36·44.

K. C. BARRINGTON (SURREY). Had the ill-luck, like Hutton, to make a duck in his first innings in Test cricket. That did not prevent his selection for the second Test Match at Lord's, in which he was top scorer with 34 towards that wretched English first innings of 133. As a reward for those services he was promptly dropped and did not play for the rest of the series.

Barrington is a young cricketer who was capped for Surrey in the same season as he earned his cap for England. There is not the slightest doubt that much more will be heard of him in the near future despite his disappearance from the last three Tests of the recent series.

Test averages:

> *Two matches, three innings, no not-out innings, 52 runs, highest score 34, average 17·33.*

A. V. BEDSER (SURREY). Manchester gave Bedser the same sort of welcome as Kennington Oval might when he made his only Test Match appearance of the season. Bedser is liked in the North equally with the South. This time he came into the side because of injury to Statham.

As at Brisbane last winter, so now, he was unfortunate in running into a match of tall scoring by the opposition. He took the wickets of Waite and Winslow, but only after each of them had scored a century. As in Australia, too, he was unfortunate in catches missed off his bowling.

In the South African second innings he had two much cheaper wickets—taken during a victory rush by his opponents. Maybe this was Bedser's last Test Match. Even if he never bowled another ball for country or County he would have just cause to look back on his long career with pride.

Test averages:

> *Batting: One match, two innings of one and three.*
>
> *Bowling: 41 overs, 3 maidens, 153 runs, 4 wickets, average 38·25.*

D. B. CLOSE (YORKSHIRE). Was restored to Test cricket at the Oval after a long period in semi-obscurity. Early in the season no prophet of cricket would have foretold that Close would become an England opening batsman. But he succeeded in the job in a Yorkshire emergency and the selectors, at their wits' end, chose him for that position at the Oval. He did not do badly. His first innings, 32, was part of a partnership with John Ikin of 51, the biggest opening stand for England since the first Test Match. Probably Close will have another chance next year, for what England wants above everything else is a reliable opener.

He did not have an opportunity of bowling, because the front-line spinners, Laker and Lock, were taking so many wickets that no other was required. But he is a useful reserve bowler to have available, and in Appleyard's absence has creditable achievements for his County.

Test averages:

Batting: One match, two innings, no not-out innings, 47 runs, highest score 32, average 23·50.

D. C. S. COMPTON (MIDDLESEX). Denis Compton, had he so desired, could have retired from cricket without the slightest fear of starvation several years ago. His love of the game has kept him in it, and now he makes plain his eagerness to play, if required, not only against the Australians in the next English summer but against the South Africans in the ensuing Southern season.

Whether that much discussed knee of his will allow it is quite another matter. It may; let us hope it will, for Compton in the series just over was at his very best until the knee let him down during the final Test Match.

It is curious how often some writers have proclaimed that Compton was "finished". The story arose as long ago as 1950–1 when his batting failed lamentably, though only temporarily, in the Test Matches during the last tour but one of Australia. Then he played eight Test Match innings, the highest of which was 23. His runs numbered 53, and, reckoning once not out, his average was 7·5. His critics conveniently forgot that in all first-class matches, including Tests, he scored 882 runs with an average of 55·1.

Compton was supposed to be "finished", yet four years later he returned to Australia again, scored in Test Matches 191 runs in seven innings (twice not out) with a vastly different average of 38·2.

In the recent series against South Africa he was second only to Peter May, scoring 492 runs at 54·66. How silly it is, then, to assume that Compton's Test career is over. It *may* be so. One never can tell how the knee will behave, but do not let us write him off until he and we are certain. Compton on two or three occasions has had to stand down from Test Matches because of the knee, but only once, at the Oval recently, has he had to remain off the field for an innings for this cause in a game in which he has actually played. Look at Compton's achievements against the South Africans, to whom, by the way, he has close relationship through marriage. No one, not even May, has been so unfailing in supplying runs—eight innings, all of real value to the side, 27, 20, 69, 158, 71, 61, 26, 30, 30.

The 71 he scored in the second innings at Manchester was, in my opinion, the best innings played by anyone of either side in the whole series. Compton has retained very much of his old daring unorthodoxy but has gained as well in his defensive qualities. He is more a man for a crisis now even than when making many more runs.

It is unfortunate that his last innings was played under handicap, for the last innings one is apt to remember most clearly. His 30 towards a partnership of 62 with May made our second innings respectable. It gave us a lead which enabled our bowlers to win the match. During that innings it was painful to watch him attempting to run; I could not understand why he did not have a runner. Some of the sharp singles he hobbled were almost embarrassing to see.

There was a time when Compton was used quite frequently as a change bowler in Test Matches. This time he did not bowl an over, possibly because his captain was afraid of straining that knee. In fact Compton bowls very little nowadays for his County. We can only hope that he will return to Test cricket next year with a knee rejuvenated. There are so few batsmen of reliable Test Match standard that we cannot regard his departure with equanimity.

Test averages:

> *Five matches, nine innings, no not-out innings, 492 runs, highest score 158, average 54·66.*

M. C. COWDREY (KENT). One ardent hope ought to be prominent in the minds of English cricket supporters all this winter—that Colin Cowdrey, when cricket begins again, will keep the index finger of his right hand out of trouble. In the season just over it was constantly in trouble—first because of a knock from Heine, the South African, which was followed up by other bowlers. Finally Ken Preston of Essex, unintentionally of course, put him out of the final Test. All this, plus Cowdrey's brief existence in R.A.F. uniform earlier in the summer, limited him to the third Test Match, in which he made 1 and 50. Even the 50 was not Cowdrey at his best. Here was a contrast from his performances in Australia last winter when he scored 319 runs at an average of 35·4.

Cowdrey suffers from a disability in the feet which sooner or later may mean an operation. He will delay the evil hour as long as possible. That trouble apart, there is no reason why he should not return to the forefront of English batting against the Australians next year. If Cowdrey had been available right through the past season our victory over the South Africans would have been more easily gained.

Test averages :

> *One match, two innings, no not-out innings, 51 runs, highest score 50, average 25·50.*

T. G. EVANS (KENT). Godfrey Evans is now in his mid-thirties, and there is a little more of him than of old; yet his ability to manufacture the catch which just does not exist continues unabated. The latest feats of anticipation and acrobatics are detailed in this book in their proper places, and there is no need for repetition. His form did not show the slightest sign of going back, and one assumes his automatic choice against the Australians.

The selectors do not seem to have any particular young player in mind as his eventual successor. This last summer when Evans was out through injury his substitutes, McIntyre and Spooner, were men of his own age group, but there are promising young wicketkeepers coming on. Swetman of Surrey, Murray of Middlesex, and Binks of Yorkshire are all keepers of promise, in addition, of course, to our reserve in Australia, Andrew. Swetman goes to Pakistan this winter.

Evans's batting has never developed as completely as I hoped. I always felt that in him there ought to be a real successor to Ames as batsman-wicketkeeper, but his batting is erratic. In the recent series his most important innings was the 36 he hit—and hit very hard—at Manchester while his broken finger was in plaster. That was the end of his cricket for this season.

Test averages:

> *Three matches, five innings, no not-out innings, 82 runs, highest score 36, average 16·40.*

Evans made nine catches and one stumping in his three Test Matches.

T. W. GRAVENEY (GLOUCESTERSHIRE). One of my most vivid memories of the last Australia tour was Tom Graveney's innings of 111, scored in 166 minutes, with 14 boundaries, as opener with Hutton in the last Test Match at Sydney. This innings was second to none played by either side in the struggle for the Ashes.

In the series against South Africa just over Graveney has not lived up to that tremendous standard; yet he has not been a failure. His nine innings have been 42—part of a stand of 91 with Kenyon—15, 60, 0, 1, 10, 36, 13 and 42. The first five times he was opening the innings, then he dropped down the list, next he was promoted again and finally batted twice further down. The selectors obviously feel that there are tremendous possibilities in Graveney or they would not go on playing him season after season. Against South Africa he was modestly successful apart from the third Test Match in which his nought and one must have nearly cost him his place.

Some lapse of concentration, I feel, must cause him to squander his wicket when his innings looks most promising. Otherwise we should not see so many scores from him reaching the thirties, forties and fifties, but going no further.

At a time when top-class slip fielders are difficult to find Graveney has developed himself in this position. After Evans was injured at Manchester he took over the position of wicket-keeper. He did what was required of him in standing a long way back to the fast bowling and stopping the ball so assiduously that he hurt his own hand in the process.

Graveney is a most likeable character, and one wishes for him and for England that his 1956 season will be a bumper.

Test averages :

> *Five matches, nine innings, no not-out innings, 219 runs, highest score 60, average 24·33.*

J. T. IKIN (LANCASHIRE). Jack Ikin, who had not played in a Test Match since 1952, was brought into the side as opening batsman for the last Test Match. He and Close gave England a respectable start in the first innings, scoring 51 together, but he was out for a duck in the second. I should say it is unlikely that Ikin will be the answer to the cry for a new England opener, for he is 37 years of age.

He is a courageous left-hander, a tremendous fighter as a batsman, and one of the best close-to-the-wicket fieldsmen we possess. Now and then Ikin bowls some useful overs of right-hand leg-breaks, but he was not needed at the Oval.

Test averages :

> *One match, two innings, no not-out innings, 17 runs, highest score 17, average 8·50.*

D. J. INSOLE (ESSEX). Year after year the captain of Essex goes on scoring prolifically. In the season just over, for instance, he was the first to reach 2000 runs, yet he has never found regular favour with the England selectors. His choice for the Leeds Test Match was only his second appearance for England. His first innings of three runs, scored laboriously while batsmen were falling all round him, did him no great credit, but his second knock was a vast improvement.

Compton's knee was "touchy" that night and Insole replaced him as our number four, and with May put on 101 runs. He looked a different batsman altogether then from three days before. In the general shuffling of the side for the last Test Match he was a sufferer and returned to

L

Essex to make abundant runs. He is not regarded as the complete stylist, but does that matter when he makes many centuries?

Test averages :

> *One match, two innings, no not-out innings, 50 runs, highest score 47, average 25·00.*

D. KENYON (WORCESTERSHIRE). Season after season Kenyon's batting remains a mystery. Runs flow from him in spate while he is playing for his County, but his performances for his country do not match this pattern. In the season just over his 58 and 32 against the South Africans at Worcester in the first match of the tour were followed by lots of fine innings for his County. This record, strengthened by favourable opinion expressed in the newspapers, led the selectors to give him a place as opening batsman in the first three Test Matches.

At Nottingham he began well with 87, and his partnership with Graveney there of 91 was the highest opening effort by any English batsmen throughout the series. After that what? In the second Test 1 and 2, in the third 5 and 1, and then no more was seen of him in the England side.

He was a diligent and efficient outfielder and ended the match at Lord's in England's favour with two well-judged catches which dropped on him from the sky.

Kenyon had played three Test Matches in India in 1951–2, and two against Australia in 1953. The frequently expressed view has been that he is "temperamentally unsuited"—whatever that may mean—to Test play. That is a glib phrase easy to coin, but I see no evidence of "nerves" in his batting, whether for England or anyone else. I give it up.

Test averages :

> *Three matches, five innings, no not-out innings, 96 runs, highest score 87, average 19·20.*

J. C. LAKER (SURREY). The selectors were long in calling on Jim Laker; indeed the last Test was his first. In the meanwhile they had played Appleyard, injured after the first match, and Titmus, and had experimented with two slow left-handers and no off-breaker at all. In the match he did play, on his own spin-taking Oval wicket, this Yorkshire-man-turned-Southerner did extremely well. Indeed, he and Lock repeated their success of two years earlier against Australia in the victorious Ashes match. Against South Africa in the second innings he not only took the wickets of Endean, McLean, Cheetham, Waite and Heine, but did so with the strictest regard for economy.

His burst of successes with Lock when four wickets were taken in 18 balls for five runs is elsewhere described. It is not too much to say that the two Surrey redoubtables won the match for us. A triumph for Laker, coming back to Test cricket at 33 after being left at home during the Australian tour.

Test averages:

Batting: One match, two innings, no not-out innings, 14 runs, highest score 12, average 7·00.

Bowling: Overs 60·4, maidens 31, runs 84, wickets 7, average 12·00.

P. J. LOADER (SURREY). In the lean years of English fast bowling just after the war Peter Loader would have found a constant place in the England Test side. Nowadays he is slightly overshadowed by the redoubtable pair Statham and Tyson. He found a place in the side only in the fourth Test Match, when Tyson was away injured.

It was no bad show that he put up, for in South Africa's first innings he took the wickets of McGlew, Goddard, Keith and McLean. It was due mainly to him that five South African batsmen were out for 38. In the second innings he could not take a wicket.

In the fifth Test Match Tyson was again away, but this time Bailey did duty as an opening bowler with Statham, and Loader lost his place. He is a good energetic outfielder with a long and accurate throw.

Test averages:

Batting: Two innings each of nought not out.

Bowling: 48 overs, 16 maidens, 119 runs, 4 wickets, average 29·75.

G. A. R. LOCK (Surrey). It is difficult to dis-associate the efforts of Lock from those of Laker, so often have they played havoc together from opposite ends in Surrey and England cricket. In this series Lock, unaccountably left out of the first two Tests, was given a place in the remaining three.

Apart from his skill as a bowler, Lock is, I think, the most whole-heartedly aggressive cricketer I know. No catch is too difficult for him to try; no ball too wide of him that he will not throw himself at it; no hit so distant he will not give chase. His very presence in any position near the wicket must be a thorn in the side of opposing batsmen. They never know where he will bob up next.

His running out of Heine off the last ball of the second day of the Oval Test Match was an example. That day he had bowled 22 overs in the extreme heat, but off he went after the ball, seized it far out, threw in accurately and ran the batsman out for daring to attempt a third run.

Lock is developing as a useful batsman; indeed four of his six innings reached double figures and some of them were extremely valuable to his side. His best bowling feats was the four for 39 and four for 62 in the final Test Match; he shared with Laker chief honours on the last day of that game.

Test averages:

    Batting: Three matches, six innings, once not out, 79 runs, highest score 19, average 54·80.

    Bowling: 164 overs, 6 maidens, 353 runs, 13 wickets, average 27·13.

F. A. LOWSON (Yorkshire). Frank Lowson played in only the fourth Test Match, into which he was brought as a substitute for his injured fellow-county man Willie Watson. Lowson at one time was regarded as likely to gain a regular place as England's opener along with Hutton, on whose style he bases his own. But since 1952 he had fallen out of favour with the England selectors. This time, unfortunately, his scores were five and nought.

Test averages:

    One Match, two innings, no not-out innings, 5 runs, highest score 5, average 2·5.

A. J. W. McINTYRE (SURREY). In one of the Tests in Australia in the 1950–1 tour McIntyre was included as a batsman. Since then he had not appeared for England until his choice as Evans's deputy for the fourth Test Match at Leeds. He himself was injured before the fifth Test Match so could not be considered again. In the one match he played he kept wicket extremely well; indeed, Evans could not have had a more competent deputy. He had been scoring lots of runs for his County as a forcing number seven batsman, but three and four were all he could muster in the Test Match. It is a pity that this neat, efficient little wicket-keeper should have belonged to the same cricket generation as Evans.

Test averages:

One match, two innings, no not-out innings, 7 runs, highest score 4, average 3·50. He made four catches.

R. T. SPOONER (WARWICKSHIRE). Dick Spooner was chosen only for the last Test Match when Evans was injured and the selectors considered that to play McIntyre would be taking an unjustifiable risk because he too had hurt a hand. His previous Test Match experience had been limited to five games in India and one with the Hutton team in the West Indies. Spooner is a good left-hand bat, but unfortunately in this one Test Match of his in England he scored 0 and 0. Tayfield was too much for him in each innings. His wicket-keeping was adequate and he made two catches.

J. B. STATHAM (LANCASHIRE). Brian Statham confirmed in this series the belief that in him England has its most consistent fast bowler. Perhaps he cannot quite rise to the same heights as Tyson and his speed is not so great, but he hardly ever seems to bowl a loose ball. His greatest feat against the South Africans was his seven for 39 which clinched the second Test Match at Lord's in our favour. McGlew, Goddard Tayfield, Endean, McLean, Keith and Waite were then his splendid bag.

He began by having McGlew l.b.w. with his second ball on the third evening of the match, followed up by taking

Goddard's wicket the same night and next day continued his destruction. England won that match by 71 runs. Without Statham we might well have lost it, for Tyson was out through injury. Statham had more wickets (17) than any other Englishman.

As a left-handed bat he now and then hit up a few resolute runs. In the outfield no one was better. His throw-in was an example to nearly everyone else in the side.

Test averages:

> *Batting: Four matches, seven innings, once not out, 42 runs, highest score 20, average 7·00.*

> *Bowling: 177·2 overs, 54 maidens, 362 runs, 17 wickets, average 21·35.*

F. J. TITMUS (MIDDLESEX).

Titmus, who had a wonderful season as an off-break bowler and useful batsman for Middlesex, was given two Test Matches in the absence of Appleyard. He was only moderately successful with the bat—4, 16, 0, 19—and as a bowler his opportunities were limited. In the second Test Match he bowled only 14 overs for the wicket of Tayfield for 50 runs. He was employed then in the first innings only. In the third Test Match his opportunities were similarly limited and he bowled 19 overs without a wicket. He was one of the best fieldsmen in the side.

No doubt we shall hear a lot more of this modest sturdy little all-rounder. He is just the young cricketer whose powers should be developed by the Pakistan tour.

Test averages:

> *Batting: Two matches, four innings, no not-out innings, 39 runs, highest score 19, average 9·75.*

> *Bowling: 33 overs, 10 maidens, 101 runs, 1 wicket, average 101·00.*

F. S. TRUEMAN (YORKSHIRE).

Only one Test Match—the second—had Trueman in our side. He was there because Tyson was unable to play. His performance was very modest—two wickets for 73 in the first innings and nought for 39 in the second. He did not have quite the consistency of Statham or quite the speed of Tyson. Nowadays England is specially rich in fast bowlers and Trueman is certainly in the best half-dozen. It remains to be seen whether he will force his way next season into the England side. He is quite capable of it if he can add accuracy to his speed.

Test averages:

Batting: One match, two innings, twice not out, 8 runs, highest score 6 not out, average ———.

Bowling: 35 overs, 4 maidens, 112 runs, 2 wickets, average 56·00.

F. H. TYSON (NORTHANTS). We should have beaten the South Africans with much less difficulty if Tyson had not been out of three of the five Test Matches because of injury. In the two games he did play—at Nottingham and Manchester—he showed that the Tysonic fury he unleashed in Australia was still available. In the South African second innings of the first Test Match he did much the same destruction as Statham wrought in the succeeding game. His six for 28 that day on a wet ground enabled England to win by an innings. In his two matches he took 14 wickets; only Statham and Wardle had as many.

Next year we specially want Tyson to avoid those stresses and strains to which fast bowlers are particularly prone. That sore heel of his which kept him out of the last two Test Matches must never become an Achilles heel. Tyson and Statham bowling together are worth more than double either of them separately. They play so beautifully into each other's hands.

Test averages:

Batting: Two matches, three innings, no not-out innings, 10 runs, highest score 8, average 3·33.

Bowling: 103 overs, 19 maidens, 258 runs, 14 wickets, average 18·42.

J. H. WARDLE (YORKSHIRE). England's selectors are invariably puzzled to know whether to make Johnny Wardle or Tony Lock the team's slow left-hander. Each finds favour at times at the expense of the other. In the recent series Wardle was picked for the first and second Tests; Lock for the third and fifth and both for the fourth.

As an attacking bowler, particularly on a drying or crumbling wicket, Lock is probably superior; but under good conditions Wardle's ability to bowl unending overs at small cost is invaluable. Look, for instance, at the second innings of the first Test Match, when Wardle bowled 29 overs at a mere fraction over one run off each. He is quite tireless. His use of the "chinaman" lends variety to our bowling and he bowls it very accurately.

As a fieldsman he is good, though not as good as his Surrey rival. In his cheerful way he made some quick runs, notably his 24 in six hits in the fourth Test Match.

Test averages:

> *Batting: Three matches, five innings, no not-out innings, 71 runs, highest score 24, average 14·20.*

> *Bowling: 165·4 overs, 77 maidens, 273 runs, 15 wickets, average 18·20.*

W. WATSON (YORKSHIRE). The Yorkshire left-hander would have been in the fourth Test if he had not been injured in playing for his County at Lord's at the very moment when the selectors were at work in the pavilion choosing their team. As it was he played only in the last Test Match, in which he scored 25 and 3—the first a very useful contribution in a low-scoring game. He fielded with distinction.

Test averages:

> *One match, two innings, no not-out innings, 28 runs, highest score 25, average 14·00.*

Twenty-five players for one Test series are far too many. Either injuries are too plentiful, form is not good enough or selectors cannot make up their minds. In any event the result is unsettling. When the Australians are here next year may fortune and form allow selection to be made from not more than 14 or 15 cricketers. In that case the prospect of victory is greatly enhanced.

Finally finance. The South Africans are taking home a record profit of between £35,000 and £40,000 from the tour. Their highest previous profit was £17,500 in 1951.

Fine weather and fine cricket have brought them this

bounty. My only regret is that so much money is always going out of England after cricket tours; so comparatively little being brought back by our teams from overseas. Even Australia, whence we benefit most, takes away from England more than we can bring back. It is of course largely a matter of population and of widespread cricket interest in this country. But whatever the cause, more money goes out than comes in. Since this exported sterling helps to irrigate the game in the fortunate countries taking it away I suppose we ought not to grumble.

Good luck to them all.

THE TOUR MATCH BY MATCH

(Test Match scores are given with the
appropriate chapters)

v. WORCESTERSHIRE, at Worcester, 7th, 9th, 10th May. Worcester won by 117 runs.

Worcestershire (1st innings): Kenyon lbw b Heine 58; Richardson b Heine 0; Outschoorn c Cheetham b Tayfield 80; Dews c Goddard b Murray 39; Broadbent st Waite b Tayfield 4; Horton b Tayfield 0; Whitehead c Heine b Tayfield 7; Jenkins c Tayfield b Murray 10; Yarnold c Endean b Murray 1; Perks lbw b Tayfield 41; Berry not out 0; Extras 20. Total 260.

Bowling: Heine 16—6—37—2; Goddard 18—11—17—0; Tayfield 37—10—93—5; Murray 38·5—20—60—3; Mansell 17—6—33—0.

South Africans (1st innings): McGlew lbw b Perks 0; Goddard c Yarnold b Berry 47; Waite b Berry 36; Endean c Yarnold b Jenkins 32; McLean c and b Horton 13; Cheetham c Yarnold b Berry 4; Winslow b Berry 37; Murray b Horton 3; Mansell not out 14; Tayfield c Kenyon b Berry 5; Heine c Horton b Jenkins 14. Extras 4. Total 209.

Bowling: Perks 11—4—32—1; Whitehead 8—1—21—0; Jenkins 22·4—2—65—2; Berry 30—11—60—5; Horton 7—1—27—2.

Worcestershire (2nd innings): Kenyon b Tayfield 32; Richardson lbw b Tayfield 12; Outschoorn lbw b Tayfield 3; Dews lbw b Tayfield 52; Broadbent c Goddard b Tayfield 10; Horton run out 4; Whitehead not out 51; Jenkins c Waite b Mansell 16; Yarnold c Tayfield b Heine 1; Perks b Heine 16; Berry b Heine 0. Extras 12. Total 209.

Bowling: Heine 17·5—3—45—3; Goddard 19—11—32—0; Tayfield 30—9—81—5; Murray 8—3—15—0; Mansell 12—5—24—1.

South Africans (2nd innings): McGlew b Horton 46; Goddard b Horton 23; Waite b Berry 3; Endean c Jenkins b Horton 17; McLean lbw b Horton 4; Cheetham lbw b Horton 13; Winslow c Dews b Horton 0; Murray b Horton 9; Mansell lbw b Horton 11; Tayfield b Horton 6; Heine not out 1. Extras 10. Total 143.

Bowling: Perks 5—0—18—0; Whitehead 4—1—17—0; Jenkins 6—3—15—0; Berry 20—11—27—1; Horton 21·5—6—56—9; Outschoorn 1—1—0—0.

v. DERBYSHIRE at Derby, 11th, 12th, 13th May. Match drawn. No play on third day. Rain.

Derbyshire (1st innings): Hamer st Waite b Tayfield 47; Kelly lbw b Goddard 24; Lee b Goddard 2; Revill b Adcock 22; Carr b Heine 19; Johnson b Adcock 3; Morgan b Heine 1; Dawkes b Tayfield 19; Gladwin not out 12; Smith b Tayfield 0; Jackson c Duckworth b Tayfield 20. Extras 10. Total 179.

Bowling: Heine 24—6—50—2; Adcock 17—4—39—2; Tayfield 26·2—8—61—4; Goddard 15—6—19—2.

South Africans (1st innings): McGlew c Dawkes b Morgan 23; Goddard c Carr b Morgan 5; Waite lbw b Jackson 19; Tayfield b Jackson 6; Endean c Dawkes b Morgan 15; McLean run out 6; Duckworth not out 14; Keith c Carr b Gladwin 6; Winslow c Lee b Gladwin 13; Heine lbw b Jackson 3; Adcock c Morgan b Gladwin 1. Extras 2. Total 113.

Bowling: Jackson 24—8—37—3; Gladwin 26·3—12—26—3; Morgan 19—6—40—3; Smith 5—1—8—0.

Derbyshire (2nd innings): Hamer c Waite b Adcock 24; Kelly not out 35; Lee b Adcock 0; Revill c Winslow b Heine 7; Carr c Waite b Adcock 0; Johnson not out 30. Extras 4. Total (4 wickets) 100.

Bowling: Heine 12—3—24—1; Adcock 11—4—20—3; Tayfield 16—5—23—0; Goddard 10—3—18—0; Keith 11—4—11—0.

v. NOTTINGHAMSHIRE at Nottingham 14th, 16th, 17th May. Drawn. No play on last day. Rain.

South Africans (1st innings): McGlew c Rowe b Smales 88; Goddard b Dooland 12; Waite c and b Harvey 30; McLean b Smales 0; Endean b Smales 78; Cheetham lbw b Jepson 22; Keith b Dooland 8; Fuller b Dooland 0; Tayfield c Jepson b Dooland 10; Smith c Martin b Dooland 9; Adcock not out 1. Extras 14. Total 272.

Bowling: Jepson 28—11—50—1; Smales 40—18—55—3; Dooland 33·2—8—94—5; Harvey 24—12—52—1; Stocks 4—1—7—0.

Notts (1st innings): Simpson c Goddard b Smith 57; Clay c and b Tayfield 15; Poole c Waite b Smith 25; Hardstaff b Smith 9; Martin lbw b Tayfield 14; Stocks lbw b Tayfield 54; Harvey b Tayfield 1; Dooland c Goddard b Tayfield 12; Smales lbw b Smith

14; Jepson c Keith b Smith 23; Rowe not out 0. Extras 7. Total 231.

Bowling: Adcock 12—5—24—0; Fuller 6—2—14—0; Goddard 4—1—5—0; Keith 7—2—16—0; Tayfield 39—14—95—5; Smith 27·2—7—70—5.

South Africans (2nd innings): McGlew not out 24; Goddard not out 24. Extras 6. Total (no wicket) 54.

Bowling: Jepson 5—2—14—0; Smales 8—2—11—0; Dooland 9—3—23—0.

v. CAMBRIDGE UNIVERSITY at Cambridge, 18th, 19th, 20th May. Drawn.

South Africans (1st innings): McGlew b Singh 85; Waite c Parsons b Singh 78; Duckworth st Melluish b Goonesena 15; Endean c Parsons b C. S. Smith 24; Winslow st Melluish b Goonesena 0; Cheetham c Pretlove b C. S. Smith 23; Murray b D. J. Smith 5; Fuller c O'Brien b Singh 7; Tayfield b Singh 1; Smith not out 4; Heine b Singh 12. Extras 14. Total 268.

Bowling: C. S. Smith 22—11—36—2; D. J. Smith 19—3—50—1; Singh 28·4—6—73—5; Goonesena 24—2—74—2; Pretlove 2—0—21—0.

Cambridge University (1st innings): Silk b Smith 15; O'Brien st Duckworth b Smith 25; Parsons c Waite b Smith 1; Singh run out 0; Lumsden c and b Tayfield 9; Knightley-Smith c Heine b Tayfield 6; Pretlove b Tayfield 0; C. S. Smith b Heine 1; Goonesena lbw b Heine 8; Melluish b Tayfield 0; D. J. Smith not out 0. Extras 2. Total 67.

Bowling: Heine 17—8—17—2; Fuller 9—5—8—0; Tayfield 22·2—8—31—4; Smith 12—6—9—3.

Cambridge University (2nd innings): Silk c Cheetham b Fuller 54; O'Brien c Waite b Tayfield 0; Parsons c Cheetham b Tayfield 11; Singh c Waite b Fuller 20; Lumsden b Tayfield 5; Knightley-Smith b Fuller 5; C. S. Smith c Heine b Smith 17; Goonesena lbw b Tayfield 31; Melluish not out 0. Extras 2. Total (8 wickets) 154.

D. J. Smith did not bat.

Bowling: Heine 20—10—32—0; Fuller 21—12—24—3; Tayfield 44—23—51—4; Smith 17—7—33—1; Murray 11—6—12—0.

v. M.C.C. at Lord's, 21st, 23rd, 24th May. South Africans won by 93 runs.

South Africans (1st innings): Goddard b Titmus 19; Waite c Close b Titmus 16; Keith c Berry b Loader 21; Endean st Andrew b Berry 20; McLean lbw b Loader 4; Cheetham c Graveney b

Berry 38; Winslow c Andrew b Close 25; Murray c Andrew b Bailey 9; Fuller c Graveney b Bailey 5; Tayfield not out 20; Smith not out 0. Extras 8. Total (9 wickets dec.) 185.

Bowling: Loader 20—8—45—2; Bailey 13—4—29—2; Titmus 20—11—27—2; Berry 23·5—10—28—2; Close 19—6—48—1.

M.C.C. (1st innings): Hutton retired ill 2; Graveney c Winslow b Murray 1; Parks c Fuller b Goddard 15; Barrington lbw b Goddard 3; D. Compton c Endean b Smith 25; Close b Fuller 0; Bailey c McLean b Smith 19; Titmus lbw b Tayfield 1; Andrew b Tayfield 7; Loader c Endean b Smith 3; Berry not out 2. Extras 9. Total 87.

Bowling: Fuller 9—2—20—1; Goddard 12—5—19—2; Tayfield 16·2—9—13—2; Murray 3—1—5—1; Smith 16—6—21—3.

South Africans (2nd innings): Goddard c Andrew b Bailey 1; Waite b Titmus 27; Keith c Titmus b Bailey 22; Endean b Titmus 4; McLean lbw b Titmus 85; Cheetham c Andrew b Titmus 29; Winslow c Andrew b Titmus 11; Murray b Titmus 0; Fuller c and b Titmus 0; Tayfield b Titmus 0; Smith not out 1. Extras 4. Total 184.

Bowling: Loader 14—5—32—0; Bailey 14—6—28—2; Titmus 23·1—7—43—8; Berry 23—10—43—0; Close 8—0—24—0; Compton 1—0—10—0.

M.C.C. (2nd innings): Hutton absent ill 0; Graveney c Goddard b Smith 34; Parks c Keith b Smith 30; Barrington lbw b Goddard 27; D. Compton run out 20; Close c Waite b Fuller 13; Bailey c Murray b Tayfield 14; Titmus lbw b Tayfield 3; Andrew c Waite b Smith 4; Loader not out 29; Berry c Waite b Smith 8. Extras 7. Total 189.

Bowling: Fuller 10—6—12—1; Goddard 16—4—40—1; Tayfield 29—10—54—2; Smith 23·4—4—76—4.

v. OXFORD UNIVERSITY at Oxford, 25th, 26th, 27th May. South Africans won by an innings and 137.

South Africans (1st innings): McGlew c Smith b Allan 66; Goddard c Williams b Jowett 121; Waite run out 13; Keith c Walton b Jowett 19; McLean b Phillips 67; Duckworth b Phillips 0; Winslow c Jowett b Phillips 60; Cheetham c Gibson b Jowett 24; Murray not out 36; Heine not out 18. Total (8 wickets declared) 434. Smith did not bat.

Bowling: Arenhold 12—2—28—0; Phillips 25—2—87—3; Fellows-Smith 20—3—86—0; Jowett 33—9—101—3; Allan 25—7—87—1; Gibson 6—0—33—0.

Oxford University (1st innings): M. J. K. Smith b Goddard 4;

Allan c Waite b Heine 3; Walton c Duckworth b Heine 22; Williams b Heine 0; Delisle c Duckworth b Heine 13; Gibson c Goddard b Heine 0; Fellows-Smith c Cheetham b Smith 28; Walshe b Murray 11; Arenhold st Duckworth b Smith 2; Jowett b Smith 0; Phillips not out 0. Extras 7. Total 90.

Bowling: Heine 17—9—31—5; Goddard 7—4—11—1; McGlew 1—0—4—0; Murray 12·5—2—24—1; Smith 4—1—13—3.

Oxford University (2nd innings): M. J. K. Smith c Murray b Keith 33; Allan c Keith b Murray 10; Walton c Winslow b Keith 21; Williams b Smith 19; Delisle run out 32; Gibson c Waite b Goddard 14; Fellows-Smith lbw b Keith 40; Walshe c Duckworth b Heine 20; Arenhold c Waite b Keith 6; Jowett c Keith b Goddard 9; Phillips not out 1. Extras 2. Total 207.

Bowling: Heine 29—13—52—1; Goddard 18·2—7—27—2; Murray 13—10—15—1; Smith 24—10—52—1; Keith 41—24—60—4.

v. GLAMORGAN at Cardiff, 28th, 30th, 31st May. Match drawn. No play on first day. Rain.

Glamorgan (1st innings): Parkhouse c Waite b Fuller 62; Jones c Adcock b Tayfield 27; Hedges st Waite b Mansell 58; Pressdee lbw b Fuller 1; Watkins b Mansell 37; Wooller c Mansell b Keith 2; Clift b Fuller 13; Ward c Tayfield b Adcock 14; McConnon b Adcock 0; Shepherd not out 13; Davies b Fuller 0. Extras 7. Total 234.

Bowling: Adcock 17—3—47—2; Fuller 19·3—4—46—4; Goddard 9—5—8—0; Mansell 16—6—27—2; Tayfield 28—8—56—1; Keith 12—6—33—1.

South Africa (1st innings): McGlew b Watkins 53; Goddard lbw b McConnon 26; Waite c Watkins b McConnon 4; Endean lbw b Watkins 0; Winslow b McConnon 36; Keith st Davies b Pressdee 11; Cheetham not out 12; Mansell c Wooller b McConnon 0; Fuller c McConnon b Pressdee 1; Tayfield c Hedges b McConnon 3; Adcock b McConnon 1. Extras 9. Total 156.

Bowling: Shepherd 12—3—34—0; Wooller 11—4—20—0; McConnon 24·5—8—49—6; Pressdee 13—5—27—2; Watkins 11—5—17—2.

Glamorgan (2nd innings): Parkhouse not out 29; Jones b Fuller 0; Pressdee b Fuller 8; Ward c and b Adcock 4; Watkins b Fuller 20; Clift not out 6. Extras 6. Total (4 wickets) 73.

Bowling: Adcock 10—3—33—1; Fuller 14—6—27—3; Goddard 3—0—6—0; Mansell 2—1—1—0.

v. Essex at Colchester, 1st, 2nd, 3rd June. Drawn.

South Africans (1st innings): McGlew c Smith b Preston 118; Endean lbw b Greensmith 64; Keith c and b Smith 94; Mansell b Bailey 99; McLean not out 101; Winslow not out 20. Extras 7. Total (4 wickets, innings declared) 503.

Bowling: T. E. Bailey 32—3—102—1; Preston 25—2—83—1; Smith 27—5—83—1; J. A. Bailey 32—4—117—0; Greensmith 20—1—70—1; Insole 6—0—41—0.

Essex (1st innings): Dodds run out 8; Gibb b Adcock 12; Barker lbw b Smith 4; Horsfall c Mansell b Murray 42; Insole b Smith 129; T. E. Bailey b Murray 107; Knight c and b Smith 0; Smith c Endean b Adcock 24; Greensmith c Adcock b Heine 4; Preston not out 4; J. A Bailey c Endean b Mansell 4. Extras 12. Total 350.

Bowling: Adcock 28—8—58—2; Heine 26—1—49—1; Smith 38—10—138—3; Murray 30—11—65—2; Keith 9—5—13—0; Mansell 9·5—4—14—1.

Essex (following on) (2nd innings): Dodds run out 21; Gibb c Heine b Smith 4; Barker c Endean b Murray 5; Horsfall c Duckworth b Mansell 12; Knight run out 13; Insole not out 22; T. E. Bailey not out 11. Extras 1. Total (5 wickets) 89.

v. Lancashire at Manchester, 4th, 6th, 7th June. No play on third day. Rain. Drawn.

South Africans (1st innings): Endean c Grieves b Wharton 13; Goddard c Grieves b Wharton 0; Waite b Wharton 17; Cheetham lbw b Wharton 0; McLean run out 35; Mansell c Goodwin b Ikin 8; Winslow c Hilton b Goodwin 61; Tayfield st Jordan b Hilton 0; Fuller c Collins b Hilton 15; Smith not out 5; Adcock b Hilton 0. Extras 0. Total 154.

Bowling: Goodwin 11—2—42—1; Wharton 13—3—26—4; Ikin 7—3—51—1; Collins 2—1—8—0; Hilton 15—5—27—3.

Lancashire (1st innings): Ikin lbw b Goddard 35; Place b Goddard 13; Edrich c Winslow b Adcock 3; Washbrook c Fuller b Adcock 14; Jordan c Waite b Tayfield 29; Wharton c Waite b Adcock 4; Grieves b Tayfield 77; Dyson c Mansell b Tayfield 0; Collins c Adcock b Goddard 17; Hilton c Winslow b Tayfield 1; Goodwin not out 0. Extras 8. Total 201.

Bowling: Adcock 22—3—53—3; Goddard 29—15—41—3; Fuller 19—4—48—0; Smith 5—0—24—0; Tayfield 11·5—6—27—4.

South Africans (2nd innings): Endean c Edrich b Goodwin 51; Goddard lbw b Goodwin 14; Cheetham c Jordan b Goodwin 45;

Mansell c Grieves b Collins 79; McLean not out 34; Tayfield not
out 9. Extras 0. Total (4 wickets) 232.

Bowling: Goodwin 16—3—47—3; Wharton 11—3—17—0;
Dyson 8—1—38—0; Hilton 13—4—36—0; Ikin 8—1—29—0;
Collins 15—6—41—1; Grieves 9—2—24—0.

v. SOMERSET at Taunton, 15th, 16th, 17th June. South Africans
won by an innings and 32.

Somerset (1st innings): Tordoff c Goddard b Heine 0; Stephen-
son c Waite b Heine 3; Lawrence lbw b Murray 14; Wight b
Heine 1; Tremlett run out 6; Lomax c Keith b Goddard 6; Tripp
c Heine b Murray 2; Saeed c Endean b Tayfield 24; Hilton b
Goddard 0; McMahon c Heine b Tayfield 6; Lobb not out 1.
Extras 5. Total 68.

Bowling: Heine 17—5—33—3; Goddard 17—8—16—2;
Murray 9—4—10—2; Tayfield 5—2—4—2.

South Africans (1st innings): Endean lbw b Lobb 7; Goddard
c Stephenson b Lobb 5; Keith c Stephenson b Saeed 49; McLean
c Hilton b Saeed 16; Duckworth b Saeed 7; Mansell c Stephenson
b Saeed 8; Waite c Stephenson b Lobb 42; Cheetham not out 87;
Murray b Saeed 1; Tayfield c Stephenson b Lobb 44; Heine not
out 0. Extras 4. Total (9 wickets declared) 270.

Bowling: Lobb 26·3—7—72—4; Lomax 14—1—42—0; Saeed
22—4—61—5; Lawrence 15—1—62—0; McMahon 14—2—29—0.

Somerset (2nd innings): Lawrence b Heine 13; Stephenson c
Duckworth b Heine 15; Wight c Mansell b Heine 2; Tremlett c
Waite b Heine 2; Lomax c Murray b Mansell 18; Tripp c Duckworth b Heine 13; Saeed c Duckworth b Heine 43; Hilton c Waite
b Heine 2; Tordoff not out 41; McMahon lbw b Tayfield 9; Lobb
b Tayfield 1; extras 11. Total 170.

Bowling: Heine 31—11—58—7; Goddard 20—10—30—0;
Murray 10—3—21—0; Mansell 20—13—18—1; Tayfield 37·2—
15—32—2.

v. SUSSEX at Hove, 18th, 20th, 21st June. South Africans won by
9 wickets.

Sussex (1st innings): Langridge c Waite b Fuller 16; Smith lbw
b Fuller 14; Oakman b Fuller 25; Parks c Endean b Tayfield 118;
Sheppard c Waite b Adcock 104; Suttle not out 44; Cox lbw b
Tayfield 23. Extras 8. Total (6 wickets declared) 352.

Bowling: Adcock 20—2—67—1; Fuller 31—6—86—3; Mansell 5—2—20—0; Tayfield 33·3—8—119—2; Smith 11—0—39—0;
Keith 3—1—13—0.

M

South Africans (1st innings): McGlew c Langridge b Thomson 69; Keith c Oakman b James 0; Winslow c Sheppard b James 21; McLean lbw b Marlar 129; Endean not out 38; Waite hit wkt b James 13; Fuller c James b Thomson 20. Extras 18. Total (7 wickets declared) 308.

Bowling: Thomson 31—7—70—2; James 35—12—95—3; Marlar 27—6—65—1; Oakman 12—4—52—0; Smith 8—2—12—0.

Sussex (2nd innings): Smith c Endean b Fuller 4; Oakman c sub b Tayfield 0; Marlar c Winslow b Fuller 0; Langridge b Fuller 14; Parks b Keith 45; Sheppard c and b Fuller 0; Suttle lbw b Fuller 14; Cox lbw b Fuller 0; Webb b Fuller 17; Thomson c Mansell b Keith 0; James not out 0. Extras 3. Total 97.

Bowling: Fuller 22—6—61—7; Tayfield 6—2—7—1; Keith 15—8—26—2.

South Africans (2nd innings): Waite run out 53; Endean not out 73; Keith not out 10. Extras 7. Total (one wicket) 143.

Bowling: Thomson 8—2—33—0; James 2—0—8—0; Marlar 13—3—35—0; Smith 14—8—16—0; Oakman 10—3—30—0; Parks 3·2—0—14—0.

v. NORTHANTS at Northampton, 29th, 30th June, 1st July. Drawn.

South Africans (1st innings): Goddard c Tribe b Broderick 70; Duckworth lbw b Tribe 158; Keith lbw b Barrick 24; Mansell run out 88; McLean st Andrew b Tribe 4; Murray lbw b Clarke 12; Winslow c Broderick b Tribe 1; Fuller c Andrew b Clarke 22; McGlew b Tribe 18; Smith c and b Tribe 4; Adcock not out 2. Extras 6. Total 409.

Bowling: Clarke 31—5—91—2; Barrick 18—3—67—1; Manning 23—5—73—0; Tribe 33·5—11—81—5; Broderick 25—9—72—1; Subba Row 4—0—19—0.

Northants (1st innings): Brookes c and b Murray 64; Arnold c Keith b Adcock 23; Livingston c Keith b Adcock 50; Barrick b Adcock 42; Subba Row c Duckworth b Goddard 70; Reynolds b Fuller 3; Tribe c Duckworth b Goddard 19; Broderick c Duckworth b Goddard 0; Manning c Mansell b Smith 10; Andrew not out 23; Clarke c Fuller b Goddard 0. Extras 12. Total 271.

Bowling: Fuller 21—6—51—1; Adcock 27—4—90—3; Keith 10—5—20—0; Murray 15—10—18—1; Smith 26—6—59—1; McLean 1—0—1—0; Goddard 19·4—11—20—4.

South Africans (2nd innings): Duckworth not out 30; Murray b Clarke 46. Extras 4. Total (1 wicket declared) 80.

Bowling: Clarke 10·1—1—30—1; Manning 7—1—21—0; Tribe 9—3—15—0; Broderick 6—2—10—0.

Northants (2nd innings): Arnold lbw b Adcock 1; Livingston c Goddard b Adcock 8; Subba Row lbw b Keith 59; Reynolds run out 17; Brookes not out 20; Tribe not out 24. Extras 4. Total (4 wickets) 133.

Bowling: Goddard 17—2—33—0; Adcock 12—2—30—2; Smith 3—0—15—0; Keith 12—0—35—1; Fuller 4—0—16—0.

v. YORKSHIRE at Sheffield, 2nd, 4th, 5th July. South Africans won by 193 runs.

South Africa (1st innings): McGlew c Hodgson b Wardle 51; Goddard b Wardle 42; Duckworth b Hodgson 5; Endean c Wilson b Wardle 2; McLean c Hodgson b Close 41; Waite b Illingworth 19; Winslow c Close b Illingworth 19; Tayfield lbw b Illingworth 4; Fuller c Illingworth b Wardle 5; Heine c and b Illingworth 8; Smith not out 0. Extras 13. Total 209.

Bowling: Cowan 15—3—40—0; Hodgson 11—0—39—1; Wardle 28—6—72—4; Close 13—5—24—1; Illingworth 4·2—1—21—4.

Yorkshire (1st innings): Lowson c Goddard b Heine 50; Watson c Heine b Smith 51; Wilson st Waite b Tayfield 23; Lester b Heine 10; Close b Heine 9; Yardley b Tayfield 4; Illingworth c McLean b Tayfield 11; Wardle c and b Tayfield 9; Binks not out 18; Hodgson b Goddard 6; Cowan run out 0. Extras 7. Total 198.

Bowling: Heine 27—4—60—3; Goddard 17—9—19—1; Tayfield 37·3—13—94—4; Fuller 4—1—7—0; Smith 4—1—11—1.

South Africans (2nd innings): McGlew c Lowson b Close 47; Goddard c Watson b Wardle 22; Duckworth b Close 35; Endean c and b Close 16; McLean c Close b Wardle 4; Waite c Watson b Wardle 39; Winslow b Wardle 51; Tayfield c Lester b Illingworth 65; Fuller b Illingworth 38; Smith b Wardle 7; Heine not out 16; Extras 20. Total 360.

Bowling: Cowan 17—3—57—0; Hodgson 12—3—34—0; Wardle 32·5—7—105—5; Illingworth 27—9—77—2; Close 35—10—67—3.

Yorkshire (2nd innings): Lowson lbw b Goddard 5; Watson lbw b Fuller 8; Wilson c Tayfield b Goddard 19; Lester lbw b Goddard 0; Close c McLean b Tayfield 29; Yardley b Tayfield 14; Illingworth c Waite b Smith 17; Wardle b Tayfield 74; Binks b Tayfield 2; Hodgson c sub b Smith 0; Cowan not out 0. Extras 10. Total 178.

Bowling: Goddard 21—6—32—3; Fuller 9—0—22—1; Tayfield 21·4—11—58—4; Smith 9—1—56—2.

v. SURREY at the Oval, 16th, 18th, 19th July. South Africans won by 82 runs.

South Africans (1st innings): Endean c McIntyre b Loader 32; Goddard c Stewart b Loader 9; Keith c McIntyre b A. V. Bedser 16; Duckworth c Surridge b Loader o; McLean c McIntyre b Loader 151; Waite lbw b Laker o; Winslow c Laker b A. V. Bedser 13; Mansell b E. A. Bedser 14; Fuller c Stewart b E. A. Bedser o; Tayfield st McIntyre b A. V. Bedser 6; Smith not out o. Extras 3. Total 244.

Bowling: A. V. Bedser 15·5—2—48—3; Loader 16—3—46—4; Surridge 7—2—31—0; Laker 28—9—71—1; E. A. Bedser 13—3—37—2; Clark 4—1—8—0.

Surrey (1st innings): Clark b Fuller 2; Stewart b Fuller 8; May lbw b Tayfield 62; Constable st Duckworth b Mansell 34; Barrington lbw b Tayfield 5; E. A. Bedser c Waite, b Goddard o; McIntyre c Fuller b Tayfield 9; Laker c Mansell b Goddard 7; W. S. Surridge b Tayfield 2; Loader c Endean b Tayfield 4; A. V. Bedser not out o. Extras 7. Total 140.

Bowling: Goddard 20—2—32—2; Fuller 17—7—23—2; Smith 8—5—24—0; Tayfield 12·2—4—22—5; Mansell 13—3—32—1.

South Africans (2nd innings): Endean lbw b A. V. Bedser o; Goddard c McIntyre b Loader 17; Keith c Stewart b Loader 11; Duckworth lbw b Laker 20; McLean c Stewart b Laker 15; Waite c McIntyre b Loader 41; Winslow c May b Laker 4; Mansell c E. A. Bedser b Laker 20; Fuller run out 7; Tayfield not out 14; Smith c E. A. Bedser b Laker 10. Extras 11. Total 170.

Bowling: A. V. Bedser 10—1—21—1; Loader 17—3—58—3; Laker 18—3—56—5; E. A. Bedser 10—2—24—0.

Surrey (2nd innings): Clark c McLean b Tayfield 58; Stewart hit wkt b Smith 13; May c Mansell b Tayfield 43; Constable c Keith b Tayfield 16; Barrington c Winslow b Tayfield 34; E. A. Bedser c Winslow b Tayfield 1; McIntyre b Tayfield 7; Laker c Keith b Tayfield o; Surridge c Mansell b Fuller 1; Loader b Tayfield 14; A. V. Bedser not out o. Extras 5. Total 192.

Bowling: Goddard 23—9—39—0; Fuller 24—8—42—1; Tayfield 51·3—26—76—8; Smith 7—3—14—1; Mansell 9—4—16—0.

v. MINOR COUNTIES at Stoke-on-Trent, 27th and 28th July. Drawn.

Minor Counties (1st innings): Taylor c Duckworth b Smith 57; Walton b Fuller 2; Padgett b Smith 33; Fairclough c Winslow b Tayfield 38; Gautrey lbw b Tayfield 9; Collins c Winslow b Smith 6; Haynes c Keith b Smith 2; Smith c McGlew b Tayfield 39;

Leadbeater not out 30; F. Taylor c Murray b Tayfield 7; Henderson b Smith 4. Extras 6. Total 233.

Bowling: Fuller 14—2—37—1; Murray 15—4—42—0; McGlew 2—0—6—0; Tayfield 30—9—71—4; Smith 24—5—71—5.

South Africans (1st innings): Endean c K. Taylor b F. Taylor 66; Murray c Henderson b F. Taylor 100; Keith c Fairclough b F. Taylor 6; Duckworth b F. Taylor 0; Winslow c Haynes b Leadbeater 40; Cheetham c and b Smith 18; Waite c Walton b Collins 37; Fuller b Fairclough 19; McGlew run out 6; Tayfield b Collins 5; Smith not out 1. Extras 4. Total 302.

Bowling: F. Taylor 29—9—88—4; Smith 17—1—66—1; Collins 17·4—5—57—2; Fairclough 12—1—37—1; Leadbeater 4—0—34—1; K. Taylor 4—0—16—0.

Minor Counties (2nd innings): K. Taylor c Murray b Tayfield 32; Walton c and b Smith 17; Padgett b Fuller 59; Fairclough c Cheetham b Smith 11; Gautrey c Waite b Smith 8; Collins c Fuller b Smith 7; Leadbeater b Tayfield 7; Haynes lbw b Fuller 12; Smith not out 2; F. Taylor not out 11. Extras 14. Total (eight wickets) 180.

Bowling: Fuller 11—5—17—2; Murray 7—5—11—0; Tayfield 25—10—53—2; Smith 17—3—51—4; Keith 10—5—23—0; Waite 2—0—11—0.

v. GLAMORGAN at Swansea, 30th July, 1st, 2nd August. South Africa won by 226 runs.

South Africans (1st innings): McGlew c Watkins b H. D. Davies 36; Murray c Pressdee b H. D. Davies 19; Keith lbw b H. D. Davies 2; Duckworth c H. G. Davies b Ward 32; McLean c H. G. Davies b H. D. Davies 18; Cheetham b Watkins 46; Waite lbw b Pressdee 12; Mansell lbw b Watkins 29; Tayfield not out 9; Fuller c H. G. Davies b Ward 4; Heine c H. G. Davies b H. D. Davies 12. Extras 6. Total 225.

Bowling: Watkins 14—2—41—2; H. D. Davies 20·4—8—35—5; Wooler 13—4—43—0; Ward 19—4—71—2; Pressdee 5—1—15—1; Clift 3—0—14—0.

Glamorgan (1st innings): Clift run out 16; Parkhouse b Fuller 13; Pleass c Murray b Tayfield 14; Jones lbw b Fuller 2; Watkins c Waite b Heine 8; Pressdee c Waite b Heine 3; Ward b Heine 0; Edrich c Waite b Heine 4; Wooller run out 1; H. G. Davies b Heine 1; H. D. Davies not out 0. Extras 2. Total 64.

Bowling: Heine 18·1—5—26—5; Fuller 21—12—20—2; Tayfield 16—12—16—1.

South Africa (2nd innings): McGlew b Watkins 11; Murray b Watkins 17; Keith b Watkins 14; Duckworth b Ward 24; McLean c Pressdee b Ward 4; Cheetham st H. G. Davies b Pressdee 18; Waite c H. G. Davies b Watkins 31; Mansell c Wooller b Pressdee 61; Tayfield st H. G. Davies b Pressdee 15; Fuller c H. G. Davies b Pressdee 5; Heine not out 26. Extras 4. Total 230.

Bowling: H. D. Davies 12—8—29—0; Watkins 28—6—73—4; Ward 27—6—63—2; Wooller 5—1—15—0; Pressdee 16·1—3—46—4.

Glamorgan (2nd innings): Parkhouse b Heine 4; Clift b Heine 21; Pleass c Waite b Fuller 1; Jones c Cheetham b Murray 50; Watkins c Cheetham b Tayfield 23; Pressdee c Keith b Tayfield 18; Edrich c McLean b Tayfield 18; Ward not out 10; Wooller b Tayfield 0; H. G. Davies lbw b Tayfield 14; H. D. Davies c Cheetham b Tayfield 2. Extras 4. Total 165.

Bowling: Heine 19—5—34—2; Fuller 13—3—37—1; Tayfield 25—11—35—6; Murray 13—6—25—1; Mansell 9—2—30—0.

v. WARWICKSHIRE at Birmingham, 3rd, 4th, 5th August. South Africa won by ten wickets.

Warwickshire (1st innings): Gardner c Mansell b Smith 58; Horner c Winslow b Heine 26; Wolton c and b Fuller 2; Spooner c Duckworth b Fuller 2; H. E. Dollery b Fuller 33; Hitchcock c Winslow b Fuller 29; Townsend not out 12; K. R. Dollery c Mansell b Smith 4; King b Fuller 6; Thompson b Fuller 0; Hollis b Fuller 0. Extras 16. Total 188.

Bowling: Heine 21—9—36—1; Goddard 10—2—19—0; Fuller 29·4—6—60—7; Smith 23—7—57—2.

South Africans (1st innings): McGlew lbw b Townsend 84; Goddard c Townsend b Hollies 71; Duckworth c Spooner b King 9; Endean c Spooner b Thompson 98; McLean c and b Thompson 64; Cheetham c and b Hollies 17; Winslow st Spooner b Hollies 8; Mansell not out 13; Fuller st Spooner b Hollies 9; Heine c Spooner b Thompson 6. Extras 3. Total 382.

Bowling: Thompson 22·5—4—67—3; K. R. Dollery 21—3—76—0; Hollies 51—16—100—4; King 26—6—83—1; Hitchcock 8—1—35—0; Townsend 7—1—18—1.

Warwickshire (2nd innings): Gardner b Fuller 11; Horner c Endean b Goddard 26; Wolton c Winslow b Fuller 33; Spooner c McLean b Mansell 28; H. E. Dollery lbw b Mansell 4; Hitchcock b Mansell 22; Townsend c Endean b Smith 36; King b Mansell 11; K. R. Dollery lbw b Smith 8; Thompson st Duckworth b Smith 0; Hollies not out 2. Extras 20. Total 201.

Bowling: Heine 8—2—20—0; Goddard 17—10—23—1; Fuller 32—10—47—2; Smith 11·1—2—39—3; Mansell 18—3—52—4.

South Africans (2nd innings): Winslow not out 8; Duckworth not out 0. Total (no wicket) 8.

Bowling: Gardner 1—0—5—0; Horner ·1—0—3—0.

v. GLOUCESTERSHIRE at Cheltenham, 6th, 8th, 9th August. Drawn.

Gloucestershire (1st innings): Young c Mansell b Smith 26; Milton c Fuller b Smith 58; Graveney c Mansell b Smith 0; Crapp b Smith 28; Emmett c Cheetham b Smith 0; Lambert b Goddard 9; Mortimore not out 26; Griffiths c and b Murray 12; Rochford c Duckworth b Mansell 3; Wells c McLean b Murray 1; McHugh b Murray 0. Extras 21. Total 184.

Bowling: Goddard 21—8—33—1; Fuller 17—4—27—0; Murray 21·3—12—22—3; Smith 28—8—75—5; Mansell 5—2—6—1.

South Africa (1st innings): Murray lbw b Griffiths 51; Goddard c Milton b Mortimore 93; Keith b Griffiths 1; Endean b Mortimore 28; McLean b Wells 3; Mansell c Lambert b Mortimore 0; Winslow c Wells b Mortimore 2; Duckworth lbw b Wells 0; Cheetham lbw b Wells 0; Fuller not out 11; Smith c Graveney b Wells 1. Extras 7. Total 197.

Bowling: Lambert 8—3—16—0; McHugh 19—4—30—0; Wells 15—5—39—4; Mortimore 18—5—42—4; Graveney 2—0—12—0; Griffiths 11—2—51—2.

Gloucestershire (2nd innings): Young b Goddard 1; Milton c and b Fuller 4; Graveney c Duckworth b Fuller 98; Crapp b Fuller 46; Emmett c Cheetham b Fuller 12; Lambert c McLean b Smith 10; Mortimore b Goddard 15; Griffiths not out 8; Rochford st Duckworth b Smith 6; Wells b Goddard 5; McHugh c Duckworth b Murray 12. Extras 9. Total 226.

Bowling: Goddard 24—7—33—3; Fuller 31—11—60—4; Smith 21—7—62—2; Murray 7·3—6—2—1; Mansell 11—1—30—0; Keith 12—4—30—0.

South Africans (2nd innings): Murray lbw b McHugh 1; Goddard hit wkt b Lambert 1; Cheetham not out 36; Endean c Milton b Mortimore 17; McLean not out 50. Extras 3. Total (three wickets) 108.

Bowling: Lambert 12—2—30—1; McHugh 14—7—33—1; Mortimore 8—3—20—1; Wells 5—1—16—0; Milton 1—0—6—0.

v. LEICESTERSHIRE at Leicester, 10th, 11th, 12th August. South Africa won by an innings and 117.

South Africans (1st innings): McGlew b Munden 161; Goddard b Palmer 61; Keith c Tompkin b Munden 100; Endean b Spencer 41; Winslow c Goodwin b Jackson 1; Waite c Firth b Munden 16; Cheetham not out 18; Mansell not out 53. Extras 12. Total (for six wickets declared) 463. Murray, Tayfield and Adcock did not bat.

Bowling: Spencer 30—2—124—1; Goodwin 19—3—69—0; Jackson 35—11—91—1; Walsh 13—2—51—0; Munden 30—12—83—3; Palmer 9—1—33—1.

Leicestershire (1st innings): Lester c Mansell b Adcock 29; Smith c McGlew b Murray 36; Tompkin lbw b Adcock 5; Palmer lbw b Mansell 68; Jackson c Adcock b Tayfield 11; Diment c Winslow b Tayfield 31; Munden c Cheetham b Mansell 3; Walsh c Waite b Tayfield 1; Firth not out 7; Spencer c Waite b Tayfield 5; Goodwin c Murray b Tayfield 0. Extras 12. Total 208.

Bowling: Adcock 15—2—55—2; Goddard 6—3—6—0; Murray 22—10—37—1; Tayfield 39·1—21—56—5; Mansell 25—10—42—2.

Leicestershire (2nd innings): Lester st Waite b Tayfield 36; Smith b Tayfield 28; Tompkin lbw b Mansell 7; Palmer c Endean b Tayfield 14; Jackson st Waite b Mansell 1; Diment run out 4; Munden c Keith b Mansell 2; Walsh lbw b Mansell 2; Firth c Waite b Mansell 0; Spencer c Tayfield b Mansell 15; Goodwin not out 11. Extras 18. Total 138.

Bowling: Adcock 6—1—27—0; Goddard 6—4—2—0; Murray 5—1—11—0; Tayfield 23—11—28—3; Mansell 23—8—52—6.

The above match results and the details which follow are compiled to the end of the fifth Test Match.

TEST AVERAGES

ENGLAND

BATTING

	M.	Innings	Not out	Runs	Highest	Average
May	5	9	1	582	117	72·75
Compton	5	9	0	492	158	54·66
Cowdrey	1	2	0	51	50	25·50
Insole	1	2	0	50	47	25·00
Graveney	5	9	0	219	60	24·33
Close	1	2	0	47	32	23·50
Bailey	5	9	1	184	49	23·00
Kenyon	3	5	0	96	87	19·20
Barrington	2	3	0	52	34	17·33
Evans	3	5	0	82	36	16·40
Lock	3	6	1	79	19	15·80
Wardle	3	5	0	71	24	14·20
Watson	1	2	0	28	25	14·00
Titmus	2	4	0	39	19	9·75
Ikin	1	2	0	17	17	8·50
Statham	4	7	1	42	20	7·00
Laker	1	2	0	14	12	7·00
Tyson	2	3	0	10	8	3·33

Also batted: Appleyard 0*; Bedser 1 and 3; Loader 0* and 0*; Lowson 5 and 0; McIntyre 3 and 4; Spooner 0 and 0; Trueman 2* and 6*.

* Not out.

BOWLING

	Overs	Maidens	Runs	Wickets	Average
Laker	60·4	31	84	7	12·00
Wardle ..	165·4	77	273	15	18·20
Tyson	103	19	258	14	18·42
Statham ..	177·2	54	363	17	21·35
Lock	164	6	353	13	27·13
Loader ..	48	16	119	4	29·75
Bailey	142·5	40	328	9	36·44
Bedser	41	3	153	4	38·25
Appleyard ..	47	13	78	2	39·00
Trueman ..	35	4	112	2	56·00
Titmus	33	10	101	1	101·00

SOUTH AFRICA

BATTING

	M.	Innings	Not out	Runs	Highest	Average
McGlew ..	5	10	1	476	133	52·88
Waite	5	10	1	265	113	29·44
McLean ..	5	10	0	277	142	27·70
Endean	5	10	1	246	116*	27·33
Winslow ..	3	6	0	156	108	26·00
Cheetham ..	3	6	2	96	54	24·00
Goddard ..	5	10	0	235	74	23·50
Keith	4	8	0	178	73	22·25
Tayfield	5	10	3	117	28	16·71
Heine	4	7	1	74	22*	12·33
Fuller	2	4	0	42	16	10·50
Mansell	4	8	0	45	16	5·62
Adcock	4	6	3	13	6	4·33

Also batted: Smith 0 and 2*.

* Not out.

BOWLING

	Overs	Maidens	Runs	Wickets	Average
Fuller	76	19	126	6	21·00
Goddard ..	315·4	148	528	25	21·12
Tayfield ..	313·3	124	568	26	21·84
Heine ..	199·5	46	494	21	23·52
Adcock ..	126	37	252	10	25·20
Smith	30	9	62	1	62·00
Mansell ..	48	7	130	1	130·00

Also bowled: Keith 6—1—19—0.

CENTURIES

(In Test Matches)

England

May 117 (Third Test), 112 (Second Test); Compton 158 (Third Test).

South Africa

McGlew 133 (Fourth Test), 104 (Third Test); Endean 116* (Fourth Test); McLean 142 (Second Test); Waite 113 (Third Test); Winslow 108 (Third Test).

FIRST-CLASS AVERAGES

(To End of Fifth Test)

SOUTH AFRICA

Batting

	Innings	Not out	Runs	Highest	Average
McGlew ..	27	2	1,456	161	58·24
McLean ..	32	3	1,125	151	38·79
Endean	32	3	916	116*	31·58

BATTING—*cont.*

	Innings	Not out	Runs	Highest	Average
Cheetham	23	6	528	87*	31·05
Goddard	31	1	918	121	30·60
Duckworth	15	3	349	158	29·08
Mansell	23	3	542	99	27·10
Waite	30	1	774	113	26·68
Keith	25	1	586	100	24·41
Winslow	26	2	547	108	22·79
Murray	13	1	209	51	17·41
Tayfield	28	7	338	65	16·09
Heine	18	6	190	26*	15·83
Fuller	20	1	191	38	10·05
Smith	12	6	43	10	7·16
Adcock	11	5	18	6	3·00

* Not out.

BOWLING

	Overs	Maidens	Runs	Wickets	Average
Tayfield	921·2	370	1,700	105	16·19
Fuller	459·1	140	884	49	18·04
Heine	524·5	151	1,114	59	18·88
Murray	230·4	112	356	18	19·77
Goddard	714·4	311	1,115	53	21·03
Smith	354·1	101	970	42	23·09
Mansell	251·5	82	545	21	25·95
Adcock	333	80	816	31	26·32
Keith	138	60	276	8	34·50

SUMMARY—FIRST-CLASS MATCHES

(To End of Fifth Test)

Played	Won	Drawn	Lost
22	10	8	4

THE END